In P

Max the Cat, by Pastor Mike Ortel, is a brilliant masterpiece on building healthy relationships by combining a blend of real-life examples with a touch of humor to keep you engaged and wanting more.

This book is written by someone that has integrated these lifestyle principles of healthy human relationships into his daily life. It is a must read for administrators, pastors, teachers, and laymen alike. Some books on relationships are heavy on theory, *Max the Cat* is different. Loaded with practical principles that will make a difference in your relationships, it is an enjoyable, relaxing, easy read that I highly recommend.

Mark A. Finley,
international evangelist

At a time when civility and respect are becoming endangered species, *Max the Cat* is a breath of fresh care. With heart and sincerity this easy-to-read manual on developing positive relationships addresses many mental illness issues plaguing our society today. Pastor Mike Ortel has done a great job of putting skin on seven key relationship principles while skillfully using endearing encounters with a cat named Max to remind us all how to be better human beings.

Randy Maxwell
vice president for Administration, director of Prayer Ministries
Washington Conference of Seventh-day Adventists

Mike vividly and candidly illustrates the very essence of what we all crave through a cat named Max. Now more than ever, people are desperate to have their very basic human needs met.

Mike not only fleshes them out in detail but reminds us that amid frustrations, inconveniences, and irritations, we should "love anyway." If you want to fill someone's love cup or need your own filled, *Max the Cat* delivers that and more!

Mike has hit a home run with this fresh, practical, and inspiring modern-day witnessing tool that will give you a new perspective on leading your family and friends to Christ!

Rick and Cindy Mercer,
authors of *Pray Big—God Can Do So Much More!*

It takes both inspiration and creativity to communicate critical, relational insights in an engaging way, and Mike has done it in excellent fashion! For decades, theologians and social scientists have explored God's design for us to receive facets of His grace, such as acceptance, affection, affirmation, and appreciation, to hopefully be followed by the encouragement and privilege to give the same to others (Matthew 10:8). With engaging humor, personal story, and biblical insight, *Max the Cat* does a masterful job of equipping the reader for deepening relationships with family, friends, and beyond. Read it and reap great rewards!

David Ferguson, psychologist
executive director, Great Commandment Network

This book is filled with scripture and illustrations of ways to encourage others to walk closer with Jesus. We love the spiritual approach for friendship evangelism and the encouragement to let Jesus speak through us.

Bill and Naomi Parson

We all need meaningful relationships. This book reflects Mike's special ability to focus on relationships and to apply his beliefs to everybody—and I mean *everybody*—who he comes in contact with. Mike and his writings are superb examples of the value of relationships.

Gary L. Hopkins, MD, DPH
associate director, Institute for Prevention of Addictions, Andrews University

Mike weaves an assortment of insightful stories that compels reflection and response—reflection about your own needs and response to the needs of those you hold dear. This is no saccharine self-help book—far from it! It is more of a "pull-up-a-chair" conversation with a trusted friend about the most valued of human needs: healthy relationships.

Fredrick A. Russell, principal
True North Leadership Group

MAX THE CAT

The 7 A's of God's Relational Grace

MIKE ORTEL

Pacific Press® Publishing Association
Nampa, Idaho | www.pacificpress.com

Cover design by Daniel Añez
Cover design resources from GettyImages.com
Inside design by Aaron Troia

Copyright © 2023 by Pacific Press® Publishing Association
Printed in the United States of America
All rights reserved

The author assumes full responsibility for the accuracy of all facts and quotations as cited in this book.

Unless otherwise noted, scripture quotations are from the New King James Version®. Copyright © 1982 by Thomas Nelson. Used by permission. All rights reserved.

Scripture quotations marked NLT are taken from the Holy Bible, New Living Translation, copyright © 1996, 2004, 2007, 2013, 2015 by Tyndale House Foundation. Used by permission of Tyndale House Publishers, Inc., Carol Stream, Illinois 60188. All rights reserved.

To order additional copies of this book, call toll-free 1-800-765-6955
or visit AdventistBookCenter.com.

ISBN 978-0-8163-6914-0

January 2023

Dedication

I dedicate this book to my precious wife, Lynn. You are an amazing woman, wife, mother, and so much more! There isn't much you can't do. For fifty-four years, you have been the human angel on my shoulder and the love of my life. I owe so much to you personally, professionally, relationally, and spiritually. This book would not have been possible without your encouragement, guidance, and, above all, your living example of these relationship secrets. Thanks for being there for me through thick and thin.

Contents

Foreword	9
Acknowledgments	11
Introduction	13
1. My Teacher, Max	19
2. We All Have Needs	25
3. Attention, Please!	33
4. I Accept	41
5. Affectionately Yours	49
6. Positive Affirmation	57
7. A Word of Appreciation	65
8. In Praise of Approval	73
9. I Love, Therefore I Admonish	81
10. Living the Seven A's	91
11. Plus One: The Importance of Apologizing	97
Additional Resources	107
The Last Word	109

Foreword

Relationships are hard! You would think that after several thousand years, humans would be experts on how to successfully navigate them. However, a quick look at divorce and family court records, newspapers, and family dinners reveals the reality of relationships—they are complex. And yet, every person, no matter his or her socioeconomic, marital, educational, employment, or relational status, has the same relational and emotional needs. To a large degree, our behaviors are directed at getting those needs met.

The life of Jesus gives us a snapshot of people in great need and of the transformative power of having those needs acknowledged and filled in a godly way. Jesus came to provide a way out of the death-sentence existence that sin placed us in. But He also knew that humans needed to know the truth about their identity and worth since Satan convincingly offers falsehoods. Every person longs to be seen, acknowledged, and loved. This simple-yet-rich gospel is what Jesus lived by, and it is the mission each person is called to!

The early Christians drew crowds, in part, because they were peculiar. They had a strange (agape) love for each other, an uncommon compassion for all, and a drive to tell everyone about the God-Child-Savior who gave all to be in relationship with us personally. This God made the way out of sin for us, and He is so excited to be with us that He already has our homes prepared in heaven! Can you imagine if every person lived authentic, invitational relationships patterned after Jesus?

The book you hold is an accessible, simple, effective tool to bring individuals into an authentic relationship with God and with each other. If you could sit with Mike for a chat, the ideas written here would flow out of him—passionately! Take a walk with Mike, and you will experience, firsthand, what it looks like to live the seven A's written here. Sit with Mike and Lynn in their home, and once again, you will be the recipient of grace that originates from a connection with God and a deep personal understanding and practice of the seven A's in this book!

Every person experiences relational and interpersonal challenges. *Max the Cat* is an invitation to examine the heart of these challenges and then work toward something better. Pull up a chair and sit with Mike as he talks about his heavenly Father and the seven A's that have enriched his relationships. Your time here will be well spent as you are challenged and inspired to better your relationships and cultivate a closer connection to God.

Acknowledgments

This is the easiest part of this book. This book would not have been possible without the following people:

- My wife Lynn has been my biggest fan and cheerleader in life. When days were good and when days were gloomy, she was there. Lynn, I thank you and love you.
- Attorney Jane Colby, my first editor, got me started on this journey.
- Susan Robbins, my final editor, kept me positively persistent to complete this book.
- Tina Shorey, graphic designer, sounding board, and counselor.
- Donald John—led me into a personal relationship with Jesus when I was 18 years old.

The following people have also left their spiritual and encouraging fingerprints all over my life, for which I am very grateful:

Max the Cat

My family
- My children—Michelle, Mickey, and Monte
- My mom, Florence
- My dad, Fred
- My siblings—Mar, Bill, Don, Barb, and John
- My uncles—Wilfred, Wes, Ken, and Bill

Glenn Coon
Ken Coonley
David and Teresa Ferguson
Pastor Joel Tompkins
Kay Kuzma
Florence Littauer
Dr. Richard Neil

Sarah Ruf
Dr. Robert Shive
James Snowberger
Morris, Gary, and Lee Venden
Mabel Vreeland
Carl Wagner

Every secretary and friend who has advised, typed, and encouraged me along the way.

Each of these people loved and encouraged me. They all have (or had) the gift of building me up, which gave me hope, value, and self-worth—the feeling that I mattered and was important in spite of my handicaps, especially dyslexia. They looked beyond my inadequacies and filled my life with unconditional acceptance and appreciation.

Thank you, each one.

Introduction

Over the years, I have met people who are generally critical, negative, withdrawn, lonely, unhappy, angry, and sometimes suicidal. Then I have met others who always have an upbeat, positive, outgoing, caring, generous, and joyful attitude. What makes the difference? *All* human beings are born with needs, and how those needs are (or are not) met affects us physically, mentally, emotionally, socially, and spiritually, which, in turn, affects how we feel and determines how we relate to the world around us.

We all want to know and feel that we are seen, heard, valued, respected, significant, protected, and loved. When these needs are met, we feel content, accepted, affirmed, appreciated, joy-filled, and peaceful. When our love cup is filled, we cannot help but overflow that love into the lives of others.

But when ordinary human needs are *not* met, we feel useless, hopeless, insignificant, and unloved. We are often impatient, easily irritated, and quick to react with anger, and we may become depressed. In addition, we tend to blame others for our misfortunes and misdeeds.

When I was in grade school, a kid moved to the small town where

I grew up. We shared the same first name (Mickey) and had the same birthday. But in one critical way, we were different: he was a foster child. He'd been rejected by his parents and grandparents, and when he moved to our small town, he was also rejected by many of the kids. Those kids began to pick on him, and since he had a short fuse, they could push his buttons until he finally exploded in anger. The more verbally and physically wild he became, the more they goaded him.

One day when the teacher was out of the classroom, the taunting began. Mickey went ballistic. The other Mickey in the room felt sad for him. But I did not defend him; I sat there and did nothing. Peer pressure kept me and a few others in the room quiet.

Soon Mickey started throwing things—including chairs and desks. When the teacher returned, the principal was immediately called in.

Mickey was kicked out of school and was soon sent to a new foster home. Now, decades later, my heart hurts for Mickey. And I wonder what happened to the troubled kid who shared a name and a birthday with me. Sadly, I don't know. What I *do* know is that he desperately needed a mom and dad who wanted him, loved him, played games with him, corrected him, hugged him, took him to the ice cream store, hiked with him, read him stories as he sat on their lap, knelt beside his bed and listened to his prayers, tucked him in with a kiss and a hug and an "I love you, son." He also needed someone his age to stand by him and defend him.

Whether we choose to admit it or not, we all have needs—big ones and little ones. But to a large degree, many of us have not had our own physical, emotional, social, spiritual, and mental needs met. And it is hard to pass something to others that you have never received yourself. This is why dysfunction is often passed down from generation to generation. Many adults are needy, hurt children inside, who have their own children who are, in turn, growing up needy and hurt. Hurt people hurt people. Broken people break people.

There are many people out there in the workaday world chasing the almighty dollar; indulging in sex, alcohol, or drugs; pursuing degrees and power and control; convinced that more is better; and hoping it all will somehow ease the pain and fill the void. This results in rampant sadness, frustration, anger, pain, loneliness, divorce, homelessness, crime, addiction, suicide—and the list goes on.

This book shows us a "better way." Time with God is time well spent. Time in prayer is time well spent. Time in the Word is time well spent.

Introduction

Time with your spouse is time well spent. Time with your kids is time well spent. Time meeting the needs of others is time well spent. Time sticking up for the underdog is time well spent. Consider Dr. Kent M. Keith's "The Paradoxical Commandments," written in 1968,

> People are illogical, unreasonable, and self-centered.
> *Love them anyway.*
>
> If you do good, people will accuse you of selfish ulterior motives.
> *Do good anyway.*
>
> If you are successful, you will win false friends and true enemies.
> *Succeed anyway.*
>
> The good you do today will be forgotten tomorrow.
> *Do good anyway.*
>
> Honesty and frankness make you vulnerable.
> *Be honest and frank anyway. . . .*
>
> What you spend years building may be destroyed overnight.
> *Build anyway.*
>
> People really need help but may attack you if you help them.
> *Help people anyway.*
>
> Give the world the best you have and you'll get kicked in the teeth.
> *Give the world the best you have anyway.*[1]

I hope these words of wisdom will affect your life as deeply as they've affected mine. A little difference in your lifestyle can make a huge difference in all your relationships as well as with your own peace, joy, and success in life.

I recommend that you consider the ideas in this book at least ten minutes a day. And I think you will be amazed at how the application of its seven simple principles will change your life and the lives of those around you.

Sprinkled throughout the book are the names and stories of people in my life who have lived out the relationship secrets to me. It is my prayer that they will inspire you to contemplate who in your life has been a positive influence for you.

---

1. Kent M. Keith, "The Paradoxical Commandments," *Anyway*, accessed December 5, 2022, https://www.paradoxicalcommandments.com/.

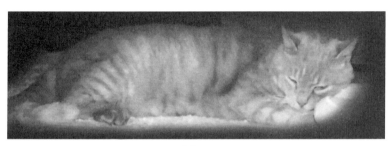

Max

MAXism

I shall pass through this world but once. If there is any good I can do or any kindness I can show to any human being let me do it now. Let me not defer it or neglect it for I shall not pass this way again.

—*The Friend*, vol. 61

My Teacher, Max

*"Now acquaint yourself with Him, and be at peace;
Thereby good will come to you."*

—Job 22:21

In December 2001, while my wife, Lynn, and I were living and working in Charlotte, North Carolina, our phone rang one evening. Our daughter, Shelly, was calling from Syracuse, New York with a question, "Would you keep our cat, Max, while David and I go on our big trip?"

Shelly and David married in 1996. They both worked hard and honored God with their lives, and they had been abundantly blessed. For several years they dreamed of taking an extended trip and traveling throughout our beautiful country by motor home—something most couples can only do in their later years, after retirement.

After considerable prayer and deliberation, having no children and being in good health, they decided to purchase and remodel a travel trailer. Then they sold their home, left their professional jobs, and calculated their budget for a year-plus road trip. All the details were taken care of—except for Max, the orange tiger cat David had given Shelly when they were dating.

"We can't take Max in the motor home," Shelly explained. "It would be no fun for him to be cooped up all that time. What do you think?"

Max the Cat

What could we say? Of course, we agreed to take Max and care for him. After all, he was our grand-cat.

Within a week, Shelly and David delivered Max to us and began their tour of the United States. While they were off having a tremendous time traveling, Grandma and Grandpa were back home, in the throes of adjusting to having a cat around the house.

Now, I must confess that I have never been particularly fond of the idea of indoor cats. In my opinion, cats are fine to have around a barn where they perform a service by eliminating rodents. But our home was in a development where there were no barns, and there was no need whatsoever for cats, so I thought.

During our adjustment phase, we quickly learned that Max was basically a house cat who preferred to sleep most of the day inside but loved to spend his nights outside, prowling about and hunting. In the evening, Max stood by the back door until we let him outside. Around daybreak, he would signal his desire to come indoors by clawing on the screen of a downstairs window.

The timing of Max's "Let me in!" request was rarely convenient. Every morning, it seemed, just as I had settled in on the sofa in the family room and was beginning my morning devotions with the Lord, and while Lynn was similarly occupied in a room upstairs, the screen-scratching would commence.

To add to my annoyance with his timing, I strongly disliked Max's screen-scratching. The first time it happened I tried to ignore him and continued with my devotions. But it didn't work. Max's scratching was incessant, and I began to wonder if the screen could withstand his persistence! Annoyed, I walked over and opened the door nearest to the window where Max sat. All I saw was a flash of fur as Max dashed by me. He swept past my legs without so much as acknowledging me. I couldn't help but muse that if Max had been a dog being let into the house, there would have been an affectionate mutual greeting. But not so with Max the cat.

One morning shortly after his arrival—and after the clawing, door-opening, and dashing had taken place—I went back to my comfortable couch and picked up my Bible to resume my abruptly interrupted devotions. Within a few minutes, Max showed up for a stare-down. He sat himself on the carpet directly in front of my feet and gazed up at me. I saw him in my peripheral vision, but I was determined to ignore him.

My Teacher, Max

I had no intention of letting that cat disturb my special time with God any more than he had already. But Max had other ideas.

Finally, I couldn't resist his cat stares any longer. I laid my Bible down beside me, looked directly into his yellow eyes, and said, "Max, what's your problem? What do you want?"

In that instant, Max jumped up on the couch, climbed onto my lap, and then placed his front paws on my chest. Even though I'm not fond of cats on the furniture—let alone on my lap—without thinking, I began to stroke Max's head and back. As I stroked him, he closed his eyes and began to purr and "knead" my chest with his warm little paws.

I surprised myself that morning. There I sat, petting this annoying cat while murmuring sweet nothings to him! Wow! This was a strange turn of events. And I asked myself, *What is this all about?*

The attention I showered on Max made him even more relaxed and content. After three or four minutes of this loving exchange between man and animal, I softly asked him, "Max, is this what you wanted? Is it enough for now?" Max immediately stopped his kneading and purring, opened his eyes, and obediently jumped down and became a contented and grateful cat for the rest of the day.

This became a daily routine that both Max and I enjoyed. A unique bonding experience between us began that day and continued throughout Max's extended sojourn in our home.

Even though I was initially resentful and reluctant, Max taught me much that first morning and in the weeks to come about basic relational and emotional needs. Our interactions reminded me that when God fills the cup of our relational and emotional needs—directly (Himself) or indirectly (through someone else)—life becomes vastly satisfying and deeply rewarding.

We all have deep, basic relational wants and needs in our lives—deeply hidden longings for attention, acceptance, contentment, meaning, relevance, and hope, to mention a few. But sometimes our irritating screen-scratching to get those needs met alienates us from the very ones who have been placed in our lives to help fulfill them. And when the door is opened to us, often we whisk right by without acknowledgment or appreciation, only to become even more lonely and frustrated, and left wanting more.

Whether you take time to sit at His feet each day or hit the ground running, busily trying to accomplish all the important tasks before you,

God longs to meet the cravings and God-given needs of every heart, both directly *and* through our meaningful relationships with others.

It took a persistent cat named Max to remind me of the importance of seven biblical principles that will guide us to healthy and happy relationships. Let's explore them together.

Isabel

I grew up in Western New York's dairy and maple syrup country, thirty miles south of Buffalo. Every weekend my mother took my siblings and me to a small country church by herself since my dad wasn't yet a believer.

There were older folk at that little country church who I enjoyed getting to know. Many of them greeted me with big smiles, called me by name, and lovingly reached out to me in a variety of ways. I looked forward to seeing those wonderful Christians each week—it felt good to be around them, and I loved and desired their kindly attention.

There was one woman I remember in particular, a dear lady named Isabel. She gave me hugs and ran her fingers through my cut hair (I had hair back then!). Then she would say, "Mickey, you are a good boy." I knew I wasn't always a good boy, but I loved her kind words, her gentle attention, and her loving touch. Whenever possible I would make it a point to find Isabel, just so I could feel the warmth of her sweetness, soak up her warm affection and attention, and hear her affirming words. With each encounter, my emotional needs were being met by someone who I knew loved and cared for me and who genuinely wanted what was best for me. At the time, I didn't realize the significance of what was going on—I just enjoyed all the kindness.

My Teacher, Max

Questions to Ponder

1. Have you ever felt like Max the cat, craving for someone to reach out and offer you what your inner being was so needing? What was that need? How did having that need met change you?

2. What are some of your needs that you haven't really thought about or paid attention to (other than food, shelter, and money), such as a compliment, a smile, or an embrace?

3. How would it feel to have those needs met right now? Would you feel content? Full? Stronger?

Something happened in Max (and in me) when I met the needs he was longing to have filled. He was a different cat when he jumped off my lap! That intentional, unselfish giving to Max the cat began a process of change in me.

Maxism

> Close relationships happen when relational needs are met.
>
> —Unknown

We All Have Needs

And my God shall supply all your need according to His riches in glory by Christ Jesus.

—Philippians 4:19

As human beings, our basic needs may be categorized as physical, social, mental, emotional, and spiritual. We need the rich love, affection, and grace that flow from God to us, which we can then share with others. If we pass along what we have received, life is so much more fulfilling, rich, and satisfying—for us and for them.

Even the most independent people—which at one time or another includes most of us—know full well it really is true: life's fulfillment and satisfaction begin when our basic needs are met and then unselfishly reciprocated. There are obvious physical needs we readily recognize, such as food, water, shelter, and clothing. And of course, most of us realize how important friends and family are as well.

My wife, Lynn, and I are both of German and English descent. We were taught that if you want something done right, you do it yourself, and you have to pull yourself up by your own boot-straps, dependent on no one and nothing else. Men were expected to be emotionally strong and stoic. I remember often hearing, "Mike, big boys don't cry," and "Stop crying, Mike, or I'll give you something to cry about."

The independent "I don't need anyone" mindset is instilled in many of us, if not by our families, then by our culture. As men, we frequently are taught to deny that we have feelings and emotions. We learn to maintain tough and dispassionate exteriors, no matter what is happening on the inside. We bury our feelings and learn not to express them. It is communicated to us in various ways that one has to "deal with it" to be a real man.

For men and boys, this denial of our feelings too often leads to difficulty with closeness, intimacy, bonding, and romance, when in reality we truly want those things. But even if we don't want (or aren't able) to admit it, we do have emotional needs. And like it or not, we have a deep craving to have those needs met.

Although women may not be taught to suppress their emotions the same way men are, they frequently encounter a similar problem. Too often when girls and women express a need, they are ignored, ridiculed, or labeled as "high maintenance." Worse yet, their expressed and perceived needs are often used against them for the selfish purposes of another person. Eventually, with the passage of time and with disappointment after disappointment, women learn to bury their emotions, too. They come to believe that if they have no expectations of receiving the support they need, they won't be disappointed. The result is a devastating loss of intimacy, trust, and hope.

In my life's journey, I've learned that when we share God's love and grace, it doesn't only make the recipient feel good; it has the same effect on the one privileged who does the sharing. That's why volunteerism is on the rise in the USA. That's why this text is so widely quoted, "It is more blessed to give than to receive" (Acts 20:35).

God's amazing grace

Exactly what is "God's grace"? How do we get it? And how do we share it? It all begins with a relationship with Him.

At the beginning of my college years, I learned that it is vital to spend time with God at the beginning of every day. Jesus, our example in daily living, did just that: "Now in the morning, having risen a long while before daylight, He went out and departed to a solitary place; and there He prayed" (Mark 1:35).

How true is the adage, "Time with God is time well spent!" Once we are in the morning habit of spending time with God, giving Him our undivided attention, learning about Him through His Word, and conversing with Him in prayer, we know we have nothing to worry about because He's in control of our days and lives—no matter what. Romans 8:31 gives us confidence, peace, joy, and faith with these comforting words: "If God is for us, who can be against us?"

Lynn and I quickly found that spending time with God at the beginning of each day gives us wisdom, humility, peace, heavenly dependence, forgiveness, power, and direction. We began as babes in Christ, but as we spent daily time with Him, we were continually filled with His grace and mercy.

Grace is *getting* a favor, gift, blessing, or miracle that we *don't deserve*, can't earn, and can't buy—such as forgiveness for our sins, salvation, and an eternal home in heaven. Mercy is *not getting* what we *do deserve*—such as punishment, shame, and eternal death.

Grace and mercy—the two by-products of our devotional time—slowly changed Lynn and me. Our relationship with God grew sweeter and made our personal relationships with each other and all the people in our lives grow sweeter too. Life was sweeter as we watched God rule and reign in us.

Something inadvertent and remarkable happens when we consistently go to God with an attitude of openness, humility, and total dependence: God's free gifts of grace and mercy enter our hearts and change our lives. Then, without our realizing it, His grace and mercy begins to flavor, color, and enrich our relationships with everyone we encounter—even a persistent cat named Max.

Over the years, Lynn and I learned there are seven A's of emotional needs common to us all. In the chapters that follow, we will describe what these seven A's are and discuss ways God calls us to share them with those around us. The premise is this: Where "great grace" (Acts 4:33) is shared, there is great power that produces great lives, great marriages, great relationships, forgiveness, reconciliation, transformation, great parenting skills, and emotional, social, and physical healing.

For years, research has shown that people and animals live longer and healthier lives when their emotional and social relationships are positive, happy, healthy, and trusting. Then stress is minimal and peace is optimal. Physical health is improved as well. In general, hurt people hurt people, and happy people make happy and contented people.

These are positive by-products of grace—favors, gifts, blessings, and miracles that are free, not earned. God delights in giving these to anyone who comes to His throne with a humble and teachable spirit and asks for them. Jesus said that His Father in heaven is much more eager to give good gifts to His children than an earthly father is to give gifts to his children who ask (Matthew 7:11).

Are you ready to receive—and to pay it forward?

Newt

Newt is a friend who is ninety-nine years old as I write this. For most of his ninety-nine years of life, when asked how he was doing or feeling, he'd respond with a big smile and a chuckle: "Fantastic!"

How and when that started, I don't know. But his positivity helped him socially, mentally, physically, emotionally, and spiritually. A positive attitude is endorphin-producing, friend-producing, health- and longevity-producing, and the list goes on. Everyone likes a bright shining face, a chuckle, and a positive word. I'm reminded of the text, "Every good gift and every perfect gift is from above, and comes down from the Father of lights, with whom there is no variation or shadow of turning" (James 1:17). Here, James reminds us to be God-conscious. It reminds us that if we are negative, fault-finding, gossiping, complaining, worrying, down in the mouth, fearful, sad, mad, frustrated, etc., God wants to gift us with something better.

If you ever find yourself slipping from positive to negative in your mind, heart, or words, cry out to God: "Help, Lord! Give me Your grace—those blessings, gifts, favors, and miracles You have for me in heaven. I desperately need You now! I'm falling into a pit of stinkin' thinkin'!"

To refocus our mind and heart on God's grace, there are hundreds of songs to sing, texts to quote, and poems to recite. Look immediately to heaven, where your help comes from the "Father of lights," and remember, "Let us therefore come boldly to the throne of grace, that we may obtain mercy and find grace to help in time of need" (Hebrews 4:16). Also, "For it is good that the heart be established by grace, not with foods which have not profited those who have been occupied with them" (Hebrews 13:9). God's got practical, supernatural, immediate help awaiting us when life and the adversary, devil, roaring lion is pouncing on us:

We All Have Needs

Likewise you younger people, submit yourselves to your elders. Yes, all of you be submissive to one another, and be clothed with humility, for

> "God resists the proud,
> but gives grace to the humble."

Therefore humble yourselves under the mighty hand of God, that He may exalt you in due time, casting all your care upon Him, for He cares for you.

Be sober, be vigilant; because your adversary the devil walks about like a roaring lion, seeking whom he may devour. Resist him, steadfast in the faith, knowing that the same sufferings are experienced by your brotherhood in the world. But may the God of all grace, who called us to His eternal glory by Christ Jesus, after you have suffered a while, perfect, establish, strengthen, and settle you. To Him be the glory and the dominion forever and ever. Amen (1 Peter 5:5–11).

Newt's life is a reminder to me that God wants all of us—His children—to be representatives of His heavenly family and to be known as upbeat, peaceful, and positive Christians. Each day I asked Him to make me a positive, winsome, infectious, happy, joyful, radiant influence for His glory, not mine.

Questions to Ponder

1. What do you think Jesus' daily devotional life looked like with His Father? Have you ever experienced a devotional life like that?

2. In what ways could a devotional life meet your needs for joy and contentment?

3. In what specific ways has God's heavenly grace/unmerited favor encouraged you?

4. Where do all graces originate?

5. Where do all dis-graces originate?

My time spent meeting Max the cat's needs (and thus meeting my own needs) would not have happened had I not been sitting in my chair having devotions with Jesus. Too often we run through life and don't take time to sit and experience the quiet that allows us to identify inner needs that can best be filled in relationship with our heavenly Father.

Maxism

Look to

people's needs,

not their deeds.

—Unknown

Attention, Please!

That there should be no schism in the body, but that the members should have the same care one for another.
—1 Corinthians 12:25

The first of the seven A's of God's grace needed by all of His creatures, young and old, is *attention*. God inspired the apostle Paul to provide counsel on the importance of giving attention when he wrote that all members of the church should care for each other, which brings unity (1 Corinthians 12:25).

Giving attention involves entering the world of another person and showing interest in what he or she likes and enjoys. The *Merriam-Webster Dictionary* defines attention as "consideration with a view to action : observant care," or "an act of civility or courtesy."[1] All of these may be embodied in the attention we crave as normal human beings, and they describe the attention we will give to others when we are caring members of a family or society.

Appropriate positive attention is an attribute of God's grace that is intended to be passed on. All of God's grace has only one origin: His goodness. He loves us, and if we humbly ask, He is eager to give us His grace to pass along to others (1 Peter 5:5, 10).

When God's grace is shared, the bond between the sharer and the recipient strengthens and tightens. Opposing views and divisions fade,

Max the Cat

becoming less important—and often disappearing.

It quickly became clear that Max enjoyed attention. He needed me to gently and lovingly stroke him, and he demonstrated his enjoyment by purring, closing his eyes, and kneading my chest with his paws. He drank in the attention I gave him for as long as I was willing to give it. Max not only needed us to let him into the house but also into our hearts.

If you have ever been a parent, you know what happens if you don't give your children the positive attention they need: they *will* get attention—by disobeying, defying, rebelling, or challenging mom and dad. And such behavior is not limited to children. Everyone knows that even negative attention is still attention, so acting out will sometimes suffice if nothing else brings the desired result. Any attention, it seems, is better than none at all.

Children crave quality time with and loving attention from their parents. They need time to talk with their parents, to be read to, play ball or with dolls, or be involved in some other activity where the parent joins in and participates in one of the child's interests. These are ways to make the child feel loved and cared for. When a child receives quality attention from a parent or teacher or other adult, the child receives the message that he or she is recognized as a valuable member of the family and society. All children need to know that someone cares for them and is glad they exist—that they have value and they matter.

Paying attention to others is basic. When you spend time with children, or your spouse, or anyone for that matter, they understand that you notice them, that you see them as important, and that you care about what they care about. It may be for a few seconds, a few hours, or a few days, but it makes a remarkable difference. Sadly, many of the children who fill up detention halls and institutions for delinquency have parents and teachers who don't give them quality, from-the-heart, positive, loving attention.

All Max needed was a few short minutes of loving attention from me each day to make him happy and cause him to behave as a model cat. In a larger way, our relationships with our children and spouses greatly benefit from our focused attention—as do our associations with friends, neighbors, co-workers, casual acquaintances, and even the strangers we encounter every day.

We all need to feel and know we belong. We all need to know that regardless of age, behavior, beliefs, social status, or economics, we are special, valued, unconditionally loved, and belong to a family group.

Consider the example Jesus set for us when He walked on this earth. He traveled through villages and towns, tending to the needs of everyone He encountered. We are told there were towns He passed through that had not one sick person left in them because of His compassionate and healing ministry (Matthew 9:35). He didn't ask them if they were believers or even if they were in conformity with His law. Instead, He ministered to them and gave them His *attention*.

Jesus even acted with compassion toward His most vocal enemies. He did not neglect or ignore them. He reached out and gave them proof of His care for them. He makes His sun shine and His rain fall on both the good and the bad (Matthew 5:45).

In my ministry I once learned of an extremely wealthy man, whom we will call Bill,* and his lovely wife, Nancy.† This couple had beautiful children and a large and luxurious home.

Bill was a hard-working man. His office was over fifty miles away from home—the commute took nearly two hours each way—and his job was his whole life. Nancy and the children rarely saw him because he was working all the time. Bill's attention was not focused on his family but rather was given entirely to his pursuit for more wealth. His income provided every material thing his family could wish for, but he was never around to give them his personal attention.

There came a time when Bill decided their home needed painting, so he hired a highly recommended professional painter, John,‡ to come attend to the necessary work. He wasn't well educated, but John was a quiet, kind, and gentle man. He owned no real estate and had no investment portfolio. He was, in fact, poor in comparison to Bill and Nancy. But as John worked day in and day out, painting that large and luxurious house, he had the opportunity to get acquainted with Nancy and the children.

As the job progressed, John and Nancy began spending more and more time together. They became friends, and then, sadly, Nancy began to appreciate the attention she was receiving from John so much that she fell in love with him. It was just a matter of time before John returned

---

* Not his real name.
† Not her real name.
‡ Not his real name.

Nancy's affection, and before they knew it, they were involved in a full-blown love affair. The children, who were hungry for the attention of a man in their lives, came to love John, too.

One late night Bill came home from the office to discover that his entire family had moved out of their home. They completely abandoned the prosperous lifestyle Bill provided and moved into a cheap motel with John. Those poor souls were willing to trade wealth and luxury for love and attention. It didn't matter to them that John was poor. He gave them what they really needed.

That's when Bill realized how much his wife and children longed for his attention. Tragically, he learned the importance of this basic need too late.

Are there people in your family, neighborhood, church, or workplace who are starved for attention? Might you offer them a few minutes of your day or a few hours a week? This is all it might take to make a profound difference in their lives. Your loving care could dispel loneliness and make them feel seen and valued. Attending to others is a privilege, and it is what God asks each of us to do: love one another as He loves us (John 13:34).

The opposite of paying attention to someone is ignoring them. But when we ignore others, it doesn't take long for divisions to be created that can be difficult or even impossible to resolve.

I like the saying, "Connected, we can make a difference." Another saying I use often is, "Together is better." As communications giant AT&T used to say in their commercials, "Reach out and touch someone."

We are all made to connect and bond. When that bond is formed, there is a contented feeling of peace, security, and rest. Max craved it, and so do we. It's as simple as sharing a smile or a kind word with someone. You can help stop the sorrow of loneliness and the pain of neglect in some dear soul by letting him or her into your world just by listening and caring.

In 1 Corinthians 12:25, Paul says, "There should be no schism in the body, but . . . the members should have the same care for one another." Lovely, loving advice, don't you think?

I know Max is a cat. I know cats are different from humans. However, the stories I've read about animals and my growing-up years with my horse, Lucky, taught me that most living beings need one another. Attention for Max included not only giving him food and water but also entering his world of nocturnal adventures and daytime naps. No, we didn't join in his nighttime wanderings, but we entered his daily cycle by attending to his feline needs. Remember, when our God-given needs are met in God-given ways, there is great satisfaction. Max did not have to devise a way to get his cat needs met while with us. When we opened the door on both ends of the day and attended to him—he became secure in knowing we would take care of him.

A wise husband

I remember hearing this story decades ago (sadly, I don't remember where I heard it). The small-town Kansas folk gathered one Sunday afternoon to celebrate and honor a couple's fiftieth wedding anniversary. The whole town assembled to honor this gentle and meek pair. They were amazing! They raised great kids who married and then raised gracious kids of their own.

The mayor, newspaper editor, and photographer joined to rejoice with the rest of the crowd. They all shared in the anniversary celebration and in a bountiful potluck meal. The editor asked the elderly husband what he credited for the success of his long marriage. The old gentleman reached into his pocket and brought forth an old pocket watch that was chained to his belt.

He said loudly to the assemblage: "My father-in-law gave me this watch fifty years ago at our wedding. He told me that every time I needed to check the time of day, I should do what was engraved on the face of the watch: 'Say Something Nice to Sarah.' If Sarah was nearby, I'd go to her and say something nice to her, such as, 'You're a great cook . . . or mother . . . or housekeeper,' and the list went on. I'd end by saying 'I love you,' and giving her a squeeze or hug or peck on the cheek."

This wise husband demonstrated the power of the seven A's. Would you join me in going forth to say something nice to everyone you meet today?

---

1. *Merriam-Webster's Unabridged Dictionary*, s. v. "attention," accessed December 21, 2022, https://unabridged.merriam-webster.com/unabridged/attention.

Max the Cat

Questions To Ponder

1. Have you ever been so hungry for attention that you acted stupid or did something bad or wrong and suffered the consequences? What were some of the attention needs you were experiencing during that time?

2. Think of a time that you have "entered another's world" and filled their need for attention (such as asking someone how they are doing, getting down on a child's level and playing a game, or helping someone out). What good things did you see happen to them and you, both immediately and long term?

Attention, Please!

3. What challenges arise when your tank is on empty but you attempt to give to others?

4. In what ways can spending time with God "fill your tank" and empower you to meet others' needs?

Everyone longs to know they are special, valued, loved, and cared for. Max the cat was longing for his attention need to be filled by spending time with me being caressed, talked to, and cared for. Are we humans any different than Max?

Maxism

We win or lose

by the way

we choose.

—Unknown

I Accept

*Therefore receive one another,
just as Christ also received us.*

—Romans 15:7

The second of the seven A's of emotional and relational needs is *acceptance,* which involves a deliberate choice to include a person in your world. The dictionary defines acceptance as "favorable reception."[1] In the context of this book, acceptance means the taking in and receiving of individuals, all of whom are in need of being loved. Acceptance in human terms means to look beyond the individual's deeds to their needs.

Typically, we focus on the appearance, nationality, language, actions, and behavior of the people we meet. We then make the decision to either accept or reject them, based on those criteria. Of course, this is natural and human, but at times it is not particularly humane—and most definitely not divine.

God accepted us while we were still sinners. In Romans 5:6–8, the Bible tells us that when we were weak and ungodly, Jesus loved us so completely that He died for us—this is *eternal grace.* In spite of our sin, Jesus offered us acceptance by paying the penalty for our sin. Even though the rest of us would scarcely die for a *righteous* person, God loved us so much that while we were living in sin and rejecting Him, with nothing to commend us to Him, Christ died for us. Friends, that is the epitome of acceptance!

It is worthwhile to behold Christ daily so we can be changed into His likeness—this is *transforming grace*. Psychologists and theologians agree that what we focus on, what we choose to think about, will eventually shape us. Truly, as we behold, so we become changed (2 Corinthians 3:18). Oh, to have the heart of Jesus and to be loving and accepting like Him! When we convey messages of acceptance and love in our interactions with others, we reflect the love and acceptance we receive from Jesus—we radiate Him.

I am reminded of my Uncle Wilfred, who was a man who possessed that kind of radiance. He loved everyone. He was a dairy farmer, and he was involved in his community, serving on the local school board. People wanted to spend time with Uncle Wilfred. He livened up any party or gathering just with his presence.

Growing up, I always knew Uncle Wilfred loved me. When he entered a room and saw me, and he would give me a smile and a wink. I felt his love and acceptance clear across even the most crowded room. When he approached me, he would place his hand on my shoulder or give me a hug. The message I got from Uncle Wilfred was clear and strong: he accepted me, and he loved me.

When I was about twelve years old, I worked on his farm. One day as I carried a bottle of very expensive weed poison that he had just bought at the GLF Feed Store, the bottle slipped from my hands and broke. I was sad and scared that I had disappointed Uncle Wilfred. But as he looked at me, I saw no anger or disappointment in his eyes—only kindness and compassion. He said, "That's okay—we can buy more." What a joy to be reassured that my beloved uncle lovingly accepted his young nephew, even in those times when I felt awkward, clumsy, and inadequate. That acceptance meant the world to me, living in a culture where displeasure was the normal response to such accidents.

Some individuals behave in negative ways in order to get attention. Others—both adults and children—behave negatively to test our sincerity. This testing may be conscious or unconscious, but the goal of individuals who do this is to determine whether our love and acceptance are genuine. It is important to remember that if we consistently pay attention and give evidence of our love and acceptance by word and deed, negative behavior and "testing" will be less likely to occur.

I Accept

For thirteen years I was a church conference youth director. I worked with hundreds of children, youth, and young adults. A young professional woman once came to my office and told me her church was not accepting of her and her brother. These two young people, like so many during this age and stage of life, were involved in testing the waters of the world. They were in the habit of staying out late on weekends, and they didn't attend church regularly. When they did attend, they would more often than not sleep through the service as they sat in the pew in a fog, nursing their hangovers. But despite the numerous expressions of disapproval and rejection directed at them, there they were, in church. Isn't that great? Praise God!

Thankfully, there was one old couple in their church who did accept the two of them, regardless of how they dressed or smelled or how long they slept in church. That dear old couple truly demonstrated welcoming acceptance of those young people. They functioned toward them as if they were patient and caring grandparents. The old couple told the young folks they were always welcome in their pew at church and in their home for a meal or to sleep—any time, day or night. They said it and meant it. Although the rest of the church rejected these two errant young people, that old couple loved and accepted them as children of God.

Years later, in my office, that same young woman, now a Christian attorney, told me that had it not been for that elderly couple, she and her brother would not be Christians today. They would have abandoned the church completely. Their lives were amazingly affected for the good because they saw true Christianity lived out in that generous and caring Christian couple. We should always remember that our actions—and omissions—have eternal ramifications.

Our daily prayer should include a plea for God to give us His grace and help us to recognize what others need. Paul says in Romans 15:1–2, "We then who are strong ought to bear with the scruples of the weak, and not to please ourselves. Let each of us please his neighbor for his good, leading to edification." In verse 7, he goes on to say, "Therefore receive one another, just as Christ also received us, to the glory of God." Oh, that the church would be filled with Christians who refused to judge, criticize, and condemn—people who don't turn relationships on and off based on how others dress and behave.

The opposite of acceptance is rejection. No one wants to be rejected. Give your life to God, and you will experience His love, life, and grace.

Max the Cat

Then wherever you are, God's light will flow through you to others. Love as God loves you, and offer acceptance to others as God has accepted you.

Jesus accepts us just as we are when we come to Him. Likewise, we are to accept others as He accepts us—with no exceptions.

Look beyond surface appearances. Don't just look at what a person seems to be or seems to be doing. Look beyond the deeds to the needs. Look beyond the faults and sins. Look beyond the smell. Look beyond the dirty clothes. Look beyond the bad breath. Look beyond the jail time. Look beyond the ratty hair. Look beyond the raunchy language. Look beyond the deformed body.

Not everyone had the parents you had, the education and breaks in life you had. Not everyone made the same choices as you. Behind every face, every situation, every story lies a heart, a mind, and a dream—ultimately, a longing to be loved and accepted by someone.

Begin now to thank God for your lot in life and pray for the person who is shunned, picked on, belittled, ridiculed, or bullied. Ask God for the heart, the mind, and the compassion of Christ, who knows all things, believes all things, hopes all things, endures all things—whose love never ends (1 Corinthians 13:7, 8).

Everyone longs for acceptance. Accept God's children where they are. That's what Jesus did. It's the only way to reach out and share God's love and grace.

Max the cat knew we accepted him, day or night, whether he was scratching at the screen door or jumping up onto my lap. He knew we were always there for him. May our family members, friends, and neighbors feel and know the same.

I heard Max's "doorbell." The incessant window-screen scratching by the kitchen door notified me that he was ready for a long snooze in the comfort of his new home. Away from his familiar surroundings, Max seemed to be adjusting well. Over time, his pattern began to change. If I was not sitting in my usual spot, he would wait until I sat down before he sauntered over and began "the stare." I think Max was starting to anticipate these moments of closeness.

I Accept

Chris

Lynn and I met while attending college in Massachusetts. I praise God over and over for bringing us together. Some say it was happenstance or luck, but I say it was providential. Although we have lived in nine different locations since beginning our ministry together, we have a special place in our hearts for New England, where we met. As I write this, I am in northeastern Maine, back in the woods on a secluded three-mile-long lake, with no electricity and almost no cell service (occasionally, I'll have one bar on my phone). This is our seventeenth consecutive year staying in this location, enjoying God, His nature, the small cabin, and each other.

The miracle of finding this haven of rest began seventeen years ago in Freeport, Maine, at a camp meeting. As I walked around the camp's makeshift cafeteria, I met two ladies—Thelma and Carol. I stood and chatted with them for a few minutes, then they invited me to sit at their table with them. By this time, I had learned their names and where they lived: Calais, Maine. It's a small city on the US-Canada border with a population that has steadily decreased over the past fifty years. Most of the wood and paper mills and downtown stores are gone, taking with them much of the remaining citizens' local pride.

As we conversed, Carol asked me to come and preach in one of the community's nine remaining churches—all of which were struggling. To help lure me to accept, she offered my family the use of her cabin for two consecutive weekends and the days between. So, I signed up to preach on each weekend in exchange for use of the lakeside cabin.

When we arrived at the huge 150-year-old church with fifteen to twenty attendees, we were smothered with love and warm welcomes. It was a high day for them and for us. There was overwhelming acceptance—and a wonderful potluck meal. For the last seventeen years, we have been coming back. It's now a tradition for us to return to that peaceful cabin and to those wonderful people each year after Labor Day.

Now, you may be wondering where Chris enters this story. We have watched this handsome young man, now in his thirties, grow up. After graduating from the local high school—the same one attended by his parents and grandparents—he went off to college. Today he has a prestigious job with the NBA in a large city some thousand miles from home. Chris' parents and grandparents raised him well. He has, you might say, climbed the ladder of success.

Most folk in Chris's shoes never look back or pay back. Not so for

Max the Cat

Chris, who returns home often to share the seven A's with his family and his community. He has generously helped them survive the economic crunch in which the area finds itself.

"I owe a lot to my roots," Chris once told me, "and I need to say 'thank you' to all who helped me. The least I can do is pay back those who have contributed to my success."

Chris returns to Calais as often as he can, where he runs an annual charity golf tournament and banquet weekend. The majority of the event's proceeds go back into the community he loves—the community that loves him back. The funds he raises are used to help at-risk children by providing sports and other positive activities for them. Chris' heart for kids is maximized by giving them *attention* and *acceptance* first, then all the other much-needed A's.

All of us long for someone to enter into our world and lift us up. We need someone to give us a pat on the back, even as the world around us is decaying and dissolving.

May each of us join Chris in doing something special for someone who needs a smile, a kind word, or a helping hand. It's a Jesus thing. Jesus always took an interest in people, especially the downtrodden, lonely, neglected, and needy.

---

1. *Merriam-Webster's Unabridged Dictionary*, s.v. "acceptance," accessed December 21, 2022, https://unabridged.merriam-webster.com/unabridged/acceptance.

I Accept

Questions To Ponder

1. Christ accepts us while we are sinners. Is it reasonable for us to do the same to others? What would that look like in some of your current relationships?

2. What do you experience when you walk into a room and nobody acknowledges you? What does that feel like?

3. What does unconditional acceptance look like? Or make you do? Or make you feel?

4. What does "looking beyond the deeds to the needs" look like to you?

All of us want to be accepted. I often walk on the streets in my city and see people who are not typically "noticed" by their community. I give every person I meet two things: attention and acceptance. It is amazing to see their posture and facial expressions change! Being seen changes things for the better!

Suppose I never accepted Max the cat who came to me every day while I read? There is power in being part of a family—connected—even for Max.

Maxism

Twinkle, twinkle little star, what we think is what we are.

—Mike Ortel

Affectionately Yours

Be kindly affectionate one to another.
—Romans 12:10

Greet one another with a holy kiss.
—Romans 16:16

The third in our list of seven A's of emotional and relational needs is *affection*. Male or female, young or old—we all crave it. Affection communicates closeness, love, fondness, devotion, value, or importance. Dictionaries define affection as a "kind feeling : tender attachment : love, . . . good will"¹ for a person or thing.

We all need to be loved; this is a fact of nature. After all, we were created to love and be loved. Ever since the beginning of time, that hasn't changed.

Human touch is an important way of demonstrating and communicating affection, even to a person who has no sight or hearing. The sense of touch is arguably the most important of all five senses, at least in terms of promoting emotional and physical health. The communication of affection can occur without so much as a word being spoken. A hug, a handshake, a pat on the shoulder, a warm smile, even a wink—all of these communicate to someone that they are valued and cared for.

When I was growing up, my dad bought a big black mare for the family to enjoy. Her name was Lucky, and at eight years of age, I was the one who developed a bond with her. She soon became my horse

Max the Cat

and my responsibility. She loved to be loved. I'd comb her mane, brush her hair, and clean her hooves. She ate it up, you could say. She loved to be touched from head to toe. What a connection we had! No one and nothing could come between us. That's what affection can do: it bonds together, like glue.

Lucky had the run of a five-acre pasture across the road from our house, beyond a hayfield. The pasture was self-contained, with a stream, plenty of grass, and succulent apples in the fall from a variety of apple trees. Every chance I had, I'd run to the pasture and call her name. Upon hearing me, she would come running for a hug and a neck and head rub. As I loved on her, she loved on me by neighing, whinnying, and allowing me to ride her in the pasture, even without a bridle! She knew I loved her, and I knew she loved me. Love gives and keeps on giving.

We know from studies and experiences in caring for infants in orphanages and other institutional settings during World War II that infants will not thrive and won't even survive if they are not touched and shown affection. There are accounts of situations where orphans had only their basic needs met: they were fed, kept clean, and given a bed to sleep in, but they were not cuddled or rocked or even spoken to. As a result, many of these infants did not survive, and those who did were unable to develop healthy relationships. The power of the loving and caring touch and voice is absolutely crucial to healthy human development and survival.

Affection is necessary for health and well-being beyond infancy as well. Godly physical contact—touch—is of great value. Through our touch we communicate, "You matter to me," "I value you," "I care for you," and "I love you" to each other.

Some people have a greater need for affection than others. I know people who were raised in openly affectionate families or come from physically demonstrative cultures. To them, showing affection comes naturally. They are the ones who always touch when they meet and greet others—and they themselves have a strong need for physical contact with others. On the other hand, some people are resistant to touching and to being touched.

We should always be sensitive to these folk and respect each individual's unique situation. Sadly, some dear souls have a strong aversion to touch because of negative experiences, but in general, human beings by nature need loving, holy affection and touch. Five separate times the Bible instructs us to greet one another with a "holy kiss." It was not only a cultural gesture; it was and is a human need. You can look these texts up for yourself: Romans 16:16, 1 Corinthians 16:20, 2 Corinthians 13:12, 1 Thessalonians 5:26, and 1 Peter 5:14.

Is this repeated instruction to be ignored? No. Absolutely not. God knows and understands our need for affection. After all, He is the One who created us as the social beings we are and with the needs we have.

It is important to remember, though, that the word "holy" is of special importance as part of this instruction. May our affection always be bestowed with a pure motive and a virtuous and holy heart. With this in mind, a word of caution is appropriate here because a strong desire for affection too often causes both men and women to make the mistake of involving themselves in inappropriate physical intimacy in exchange for affection. In my experience, a lack of affection in the home lies at the bottom of both young people and marital partners falling into the trap of meeting their needs by looking for affection in all the wrong places. We all have witnessed far too many homes break up because one spouse sought affection elsewhere. The emotional need for affection is so strong that even good Christian homes are destroyed because of the need to feel intimately valued and desired.

I have seen people far too often offering sex as a means of getting what they thought was genuine attention, acceptance, and affection. This proves the strength of our desire for fulfillment of these unmet emotional needs.

A complete opposite of godly, holy affection is unholy intimacy. It is crucial to never allow or engage in inappropriate touching or touching with an impure, unholy motive.

Another opposite of affection is the distancing of yourself from others and denial of affection to those close to you. When we distance ourselves from others and fail to reach out and greet and treat them with holy affection, we are not obeying the direct instruction of scripture. A clear "thus saith the Lord" requires us to allow God to reach out to touch others through us. In homes where this heavenly grace is shared genuinely and freely, there is stability and there are healthy, loving relationships.

This Christian grace—the sharing of Godly affection—like all other Christian graces, originates in heaven from the throne of God, from whence "every good and every perfect gift" originates (James 1:17). If you recognize that you have not been sharing affection or realize that you have been denying others this heavenly grace, whether your family members or others who God has placed in your path, go to God and ask Him to give you the ability to brighten the lives of others around you—of course, in Christ-like love.

> Here's a little hug for you,
> To make you smile when you feel blue:
> To make you happy if you're sad:
> To let you know life's not so bad.
> Now I've given a hug to you,
> Somehow I feel better too.
> Hugs are better when you share,
> So, this is for you to show I care.
> —*Author Unknown*

I believe that both Max and I benefited from his morning perching on my lap. He enjoyed my rubbing of his head and back, and he returned the favor by purring and kneading my chest. Most animals and people alike respond favorably to selfless, holy touch.

If Max and I grew closer to each other through touch, could there be a spouse, parent, child, neighbor, or friend who is hungry—emotionally hungry—for you to reach out to with a handshake, a gentle pat, a hug, or a holy kiss on the cheek?

Romans 12:10 tells us to be "kindly affectionate" one to another. May we respond to this instruction appropriately and consistently.

The adversary attacks the things that God tells us are essential for our good and our well-being. Physical touch is a God-created need, but when illness or circumstances makes physical touch difficult or impossible, there are ways we can show affection while remaining responsibly cautious. There are many ways we can tell people that they are valued, important, and worthy. Consider the following sweet suggestions:

- "I miss you."
- "I'm praying for you."
- "I love you."
- "I think of you often."
- "You are special to me."

Affectionately Yours

- "You bring joy and light to my life."
- "I thank God for you."

Along with positive words of attention, acceptance, and affection, we can communicate fondness and tenderness through gestures, such as:

- A smile
- A wink
- A thumbs-up
- A nodding of the head
- A fist- or elbow-bump
- An air-kiss

What the devil means for evil, the Lord has countless ways to overcome for good.

Our lap time for touch and tenderness seemed to have its lasting effects on Max. After Max's almost-two-year stint with us, our daughter and her husband noticed he wasn't quite so defensive and testy. In fact, he had calmed down quite a bit. It's amazing what positive affection will do!

Don

I look back to my college days—soon after I surrendered my life to Christ—with joy. I remember one evening knocking on the dormitory door of one of the school's most humble and popular students. I imagine I felt almost like Nicodemus must have when he met with Jesus.

Don opened the door to his tiny room, just big enough for his single bed and a small desk, and he invited me in and offered a seat on the bed. After a few minutes of small talk, I asked the question that brought me to his door: "Don, what makes you the most well-liked and happiest person on campus?"

It only took him a couple of seconds to point to the white mimeographed sheet taped to his painted cement wall.

"That's my goal in life," he said. "This quote inspires me to be like Jesus: 'I expect to pass through life but once. If, therefore, there be any kindness I can show, or any good thing I can do to any fellow-being,

Max the Cat

let <u>me do it now, and not defer or neglect it, as I shall not pass this way again.</u>' "*

Don was a man who met everyone with a million-dollar smile. He gave every person his undivided *attention*, whether you were an old friend or a new acquaintance. Whether your conversation with him was long or short, you felt *accepted*. Upon walking away, you felt *affection* from him and toward him. There was an immediate connection. He had ways of building you up that *affirmed* you. Then he'd be thanking you for something, big or small, and you felt *appreciated*. He sure knew how to cheer you up in an *approving* way. Because of your extraordinary experience with him, you never wanted to do or say anything that would cause him to *admonish* you.

Don's smile, his tender laugh, and his soft-spoken voice left you thinking, *What an amazing young man!*

All this didn't just "happen." Don's quiet time alone with God each day, reflecting on the Bible and what it meant to pass through this world—this day—just once, made him the most popular, loved, and lovable person on campus.

After I left Don's room that evening fifty-five years ago, I was a changed man. My prayer is that you will be changed, too, by reading this story. Just remember: we shall pass through this world but once, and we shall not pass this way again.

---

1. *Merriam-Webster's Unabridged Dictionary,* s.v. "affection," accessed December 21, 2022, https://unabridged.merriam-webster.com/unabridged/affection.

---

* Author unknown, but attributed to William Penn and many others.

Questions to ponder

1. What is one of the most powerful ways to communicate affection? When was the last time you did that? How did you feel? How did it impact the other person?

2. What are some of the meaningful expressions of affection that speak to you, such as "You matter to me," "I care about you," "You are valuable to me"?

3. List some affectionate phrases that say "you are special to me."

4. List some nonverbal ways to say "I love and care for you."

5. What are some non-affectionate words and actions you have been the recipient of? How did these make you feel?

6. Is affection unconditional at some times? If so, how?

Touch is such a powerful emotion. For every person I meet, I find a way to connect with them in a personal way. Sometimes I give a hug, other times it's a thumbs-up, a wink, a smile, or a kind word. Everyone wants to feel somebody loves them.

Max the cat needed love, and when it was given, he relaxed and soaked in anything I was willing to give. He became transformed from a fearful, pitiful animal to a well-behaved, contented cat. Everybody wants some luvin'!

Maxism

Love seeks one thing only: the good of the one loved.

—Thomas Merton

Positive Affirmation

*Let no corrupt word proceed out of your mouth,
but what is good for necessary edification.*
—Ephesians 4:29

*Therefore let us pursue the things . . .
by which one may edify another.*
—Romans 14:19

The fourth of the seven A's of emotional health and well-being is *affirmation*—referred to in the Bible as edification. Affirmation is defined as the "act of affirming, asserting as true, or confirming : a positive assertion."¹ In short, it means encouraging and building others up. Our human nature is more apt to tear others down by our words and actions than to build them up. How frequently negative, fault-finding, critical, and judgmental words come from our mouths! But oh, how nice it would be if only positive, complimentary, and encouraging words flowed freely from you and me.

In Christ's day, wouldn't people have been surprised and disappointed if they had heard our Savior speaking evil, repeating idle gossip, or putting anyone down with cheap insults? Paul tells us in Ephesians 4:29, "Let no corrupt word proceed out of your mouth, but what is good for necessary edification, that it may impart grace to the hearers." And in Romans 14:19, Paul counsels, "Therefore let us pursue the things which make for peace and the things by which one may edify another."

God builds us up and grows, edifies, and affirms us as His children as we are grafted into the vine, Jesus Christ. God is in the business of encouragement. The devil is in the business of criticism and destruction. Affirmation and edification lead to other positive behaviors that, when bestowed, may be passed on from one person to another. A wife affirms her husband. The husband affirms his children. The children affirm their friends. Their friends bring that affirmation and positive attitude into their homes, where it is passed on even further. And so it goes. The affirmed husband and wife affirm their co-workers and friends, and those individuals share the love with their friends and family.

When I had a change of heart and began to treat Max the cat with affection and spoke kind words that affirmed him, he purred. When you affirm others, there is often a similar response—you may even be rewarded with a demonstration of appreciation and joy.

Affirmation provides support and encouragement to the recipient. Affirmation may lead to forgiveness, build strong families, and strengthen relational bonding. In my opinion, affirmation is one of love's strongest building blocks.

Throughout our life and ministry together, Lynn and I have preferred to associate ourselves with friends who are in the habit of speaking well of others. We tend to avoid people who engage in fault-finding and negativity. This is not to say that we don't gratefully receive constructive criticism, or that we are not open to sharing others' burdens, or that we are not available to help resolve issues and problems arise in our mission field. But we are particularly uplifted by loving, positive associations. We know heaven will be void of complaints and murmuring.

There are many stories told by a variety of people who share that a teacher made a tremendous difference in their life. Whenever I hear one of these stories, I immediately think of God's miracle-working power of love and affirmation. There is often a direct connection between negative choices and generational cycles. After all, humans tend to follow whatever is most familiar. So if your examples made bad choices, you are more likely to make bad choices; and if your family and friends made good choices, you are more likely to do the same. This may seem like an overgeneralization, but the connection is visible to observers.

Overcoming negative circumstances and challenges is contingent on many things, but oftentimes it is precipitated by a parent, teacher, or friend who, by God's grace, apply the counsel found in Romans 12:15, "Rejoice with those who rejoice, and weep with those who weep." Affirmation can precipitate transformation—through encouragement we can

Positive Affirmation

build others up, cheer them on, and provide security by always being there for them.

One loving and dedicated parent, teacher, or friend in the life of a child or teen demonstrates that loving and "gracing" one another pays off.

Years ago, before Lynn and I got married, I remember all too well hearing a father tell us, in front of his twelve- or thirteen-year-old son, that the boy would "never amount to anything." He then loudly ordered his son to get out of his presence, and he said the youngster could never do anything right.

Thirty years later I asked my mother what ever happened to that boy. She told me no one knew where he was or what he was doing. After a few broken marriages and failed jobs, he had dropped out of sight. She concluded by saying the now grown-up child never amounted to anything. What a sad fulfilled prophecy in that boy's life. While the boy grew up and made his own choices, there is little question that his father's words to him influenced his thinking and subsequent decisions.

Truly, parents hold in their words and actions much of our children's futures. We can encourage, affirm, and build up our children—and spouses, co-workers, and friends, too—or we can criticize and tear them down and fling negative and belittling words at them. Let us pray daily to lift others up, not tear them down.

Oh, how Max loved to be built up by the praises and hugs affirming him for always coming at the sound of his name. Animals crave affirmation just like we humans do.

Make someone's day by affirming them for something small or large they have done. Failing to build someone up is, to many emotionally starved souls, the same as putting them down—even if you don't intend to, that's how they interpret it.

Remember that everyone we meet longs to be encouraged, not put down. Our words and looks are powerful tools for good—or bad.

May God's grace prepare us now to live in the atmosphere of heaven by working through us to create a heavenly atmosphere wherever we may be.

Evelyn and Irene

Evelyn was endearingly called Hogie, and all of us at the church in Corning, New York, loved her. Well beyond retirement age, she was soft-spoken and sweet. She used a walker, and her gait was slow.

Max the Cat

I remember my first pastoral visit to Hogie's humble, neat, clean, and organized dwelling. She seemed to know everyone in Corning, and I wondered why.

When Lynn and I arrived in town, a photo of the two of us appeared with a long, well-written article in the daily newspaper. Every week there was an article about whatever our church or denomination was doing locally or somewhere in the world. I was surprised at the consistently good coverage. Then I learned it was because of Hogie. Soon after I arrived, she arranged appointments for me with the local radio station, the American Heart Association, and the American Cancer Society. Then a few weeks later, she scheduled interviews with the police chief and newspaper editor.

As I sat in Hogie's kitchen chair on my first visit, she offered me some water. The next visit, she again offered me water. I accepted but told her I would get it myself. As I stood at the sink filling my glass, I noticed a plaque on the wall that read, "Loving and giving is what makes life worth living." When I sat back down, I asked Hogie about the words on the plaque. She informed me that was her life goal throughout every age and stage of her life.

Each time I left her home, Hogie gave me something to take to my new bride. She knew we didn't have many belongings, so she sent items she thought Lynn would need in setting up our apartment. She certainly was loving and giving!

Then I learned that this humble, ordinary, precious, sweet lady was invited to every gala event in the city—and was personally transported by the mayor, the newspaper editor, the police chief, or a patrolman. And of course, Hogie gifted each driver with a plate or tin of cookies or some other delectable treat to thank them for their assistance.

Why?

Because loving and giving is what makes life worth living.

Hogie treated everyone the same. She had been given the gift from heaven's storehouse of loving up on others—the seven A's in action.

Irene, another member of the same church, made thousands of Christmas cookies each year and gave them to hundreds of families during the holiday season. Hogie and Irene were both generous with smiles, kindness, and the seven A's, which made them examples of true Christianity in action. They were magnets for Jesus. Remember what God's word tells us:

Positive Affirmation

It is better to give than to receive (Acts 20:35).

The more you give, the more you receive (Proverbs 11:24).

What you give comes back, pressed down and overflowing (Luke 6:38).

May you experience the "loving and giving" principle, which "makes life worth living."

All those mornings of "sweet nothings" I shared with Max somehow transitioned into "sweet somethings" for him. When I was working in the flower beds, Max would slowly approach, rub against my leg, and even purr as he lingered for a few minutes. I think that was his affirmation for me! He was telling me, "Hey, you're doing a great job!"

---

1. *Merriam-Webster's Unabridged Dictionary*, s.v. "affirmation," accessed December 22, 2022, https://unabridged.merriam-webster.com/unabridged/affirmation.

Max the Cat

Questions to Ponder

1. What are the two words mentioned in the chapter that means "to build up"?

2. What are some things we do or say to tear people down?

3. What was the four-word sentence in this chapter used by the Baltimore teacher that expressed how she affirmed her students?

Positive Affirmation

4. Discouraging words do what to a person?

5. How do you feel when someone affirms you?

Some of the most discouraging experiences I have had included words such as "I'm breaking our long-term relationship; I thought I loved you but I don't." It made me feel sad, helpless, useless, and unlovable. In that moment, and for many moments afterward, God stepped in and affirmed me; and in time, He abundantly provided human love and connection.

Lynn and I were greatly affirmed that Max the cat was receiving our love and attention when we opened the door each morning and found his gifts of rodents! He gave back to us, in the only way he could, the greatest thanks for our acceptance of him.

Maxism

The Bible is full of promises stating that heaven is full of gifts for people who are full of needs.

—Mike Ortel

A Word of Appreciation

In everything give thanks.
—1 Thessalonians 5:18

Number five in the list of seven A's of God's grace* is *appreciation*. The dictionary defines appreciation as "expression of gratification and approval, of gratitude."[1] We often express appreciation with a simple and genuine thank you.

Have you ever known a positive, appreciative individual? Lynn and I have. Every time the thought of our friend Malcolm comes to mind, I recall hearing him say, "Thank you," or "I appreciate you." Often, when we ran into Malcolm, he would share how much he and his wife Hazel appreciated us for our work and the things we accomplished. Of course, we are completely human, so we loved that he chose to focus on the good in us. It isn't as though we don't have faults—far from it. But his

---

* Grace is a favor, gift, blessing, or miracle that we do not deserve and cannot earn. My eternal salvation might be called eternal grace. Yet there are hundreds of earthly favors we can receive from God or others to pass along. One of these favors is a thank you. The passing on of those words goes a long way in keeping the giver and the receiver positive, happy, healthy, and feeling good about themselves. The sharing of grace goes a long way in making earthly relationships upbeat and cheery. Usually, the more appreciation we give away, the more we receive.

positive image of us, as he encouraged, edified, and bestowed his love on us, lifted us up and made us better, more loving, and more encouraging Christians to others.

It is a fact that people tend to rise to the image we have of them. When we communicate our positive image of people, they will likely live up to what we see in them. Isn't that wonderful? That's what God does for us, isn't it? He demonstrated how valuable we were to Him by coming here and giving His life for us because He saw us as "future perfect," even while we were "current sinners."

When we allow God to work in us to will and to do His good pleasure, we begin to get a vision of His plan for us—and for everyone else too. He loves and encourages us to follow Him and to be the best we can be. In turn, we can love and encourage others to do the same. God's way of working is downright beautiful. It's exciting to watch, and it's exciting to participate in it.

God views each of us as His royal children with whom He plans to reign throughout all eternity. Now, that's a positive image, isn't it? Don't you want to live up to God's image of you? Don't you want to share God's image of others with them? Ephesians 5:20 invites us to give thanks always for all things to God the Father, in the name of the Lord Jesus. This keeps us focused on our good God and His grace. How He loves our positive praise and thanksgiving!

One of the most positive men I have ever met—a man who was instrumental in leading me to Christ—was Glenn Coon. I had just turned nineteen when I first saw and heard Pastor Coon speak at a camp meeting in Union Springs, New York. At the time, he was in his sixties, and he had just published a book titled *Path to the Heart*. In my relatively short life, I had never witnessed a more exuberant, positive, and appreciative preacher.

The night I heard him speak, I was not consciously receptive to the wooing of the Holy Spirit. In some ways, I was actually rejecting God and running in the other direction. Yet His Holy Spirit led, and I found myself at the back of a big tent where soon I was mesmerized by that fast-talking, fast-walking, happy, vibrant, grateful, and appreciative man. I had never seen anyone preach like him. He didn't stand still, tell stories, and quote scripture, and he didn't put guilt trips on the congregation or try to scare them into surrendering themselves to Jesus. No. His entire message painted a positive, happy, and inviting portrait of Jesus and of the Christian life—a life that is filled with joy and peace and a God who pours out abundant love, joy, grace, and pardon on His followers.

After being jarred awake by that positive and joyous preacher, I made my way to the Book and Bible House where he was signing his book. It was one of the first books I had ever bought, and I wanted to get him to sign it. But I was too shy and insecure to stand in line and meet Pastor Coon face to face. Since I was still trying to run from God, I didn't feel comfortable being that close to what I regarded as "the man with the million-dollar smile" who had Jesus bubbling out of his heart. Instead, I lingered in the shadows and thought, *What a man, what a Christian!*

That summer I slowly read through Pastor Coon's book, and it changed the direction of my life. Because of him, I did a complete about face, turning from sin to Jesus and salvation. Ever since reading that book and experiencing the beauty of Pastor Coon's simple, loving Christianity, I have believed that a thankful, dynamic Christian can influence more people for God than a room full of guilt-tripping, non-appreciative preachers.

Appreciation is so easy, a simple "thank you!" or "thanks so much!" may be all we need to say. We all like to be thanked; it is one of our basic human emotional grace-needs. May this verse burn within us and through us: "In everything give thanks; for this is the will of God in Christ Jesus for you" (1 Thessalonians 5:18). Ephesians 5:20 also tells us to give thanks. This is a direct "thus saith the Lord." Shouldn't we take heed and obey? May each of us carefully guard against ever taking anyone or anything for granted. Let's be grateful and thankful, and let's express our gratitude and appreciation verbally.

My wife and I were in Home Depot the other day. The woman helping us looked sad and discouraged. Lynn thanked her profusely for all her help, and the woman began to weep. She obviously was not accustomed to receiving praise and appreciation and told Lynn what a profound affect those kind words had on her day.

Say, "Thanks, buddy," to the fellow who rounds up the shopping carts at the grocery store. When you do, you will likely notice an immediate difference. He will straighten up and smile. You have brightened his day, and he will pass it on to someone else. Nearly every day I encounter at least twenty-five people to whom I can say "thank you." Grace goes from one to another and on and on.

Even animals express thanks when grace is bestowed on them. Max thanked me by his affectionate purring, by rubbing up against my ankle, and by not destroying our furniture with his sharp claws. A dog will wag his tail and a horse will whinny.

We are told to come boldly before the throne of God (Hebrews 4:16). That is where we receive God's grace that we can then share with others. There is an abundant supply. Not just "enough"—God's grace is *abundant* and *boundless* (2 Corinthians 9:8)!

Love gives; selfishness takes (John 3:16, John 10:10). When we go to God for grace, He shares His attention and appreciation with us. Look at the amazing grace He bestowed on us when He loved us so much He gave His only begotten Son to the entire world for the salvation of every soul. When we know and accept that gift personally, it will be in our conversations continually, says the psalmist, "Let everything that has breath praise the Lord. Praise the Lord!" (Psalm 150:6).

Love looks like grace, and grace looks like being thankful. Pass it on. When you smile and express appreciation, you and the person with whom you interact will both receive a blessing and go on about your day happier.

When you express appreciation and love to others, you become a more attractive person yourself. People are craving—are hungry for—God's grace. One way to satisfy that craving and hunger is to take every opportunity to express appreciation for the contributions they make to your life or to society or the world in general.

Jesus clearly appreciated the expression of acceptance and appreciation proffered by the thief on the cross. What a powerful example! The appreciation of that condemned and dying man was rewarded with an eternal expression of appreciation. What grace. What love.

Always let people know they are valued. Always let people know they are appreciated. Just a thumbs-up or a pat on the shoulder can speak volumes without even opening your mouth. We all need it; why not give it?

But in order to give, we need to receive. Therefore, go boldly to God's throne of grace *first* to receive so you can give.

The opposite of appreciating is taking for granted, which is soul-deadening, often rude, unkind, and un-Christlike. The one taken for granted may feel used, victimized, and uncared for. There are, no doubt, scores of people around us each day who are starved for a thank you or a bit of praise. Value them by saying, "Thanks."

A Word of Appreciation

I am eternally thankful for the people like our friend Malcolm, and Pastor Glenn Coon, whom God sent into my life to demonstrate what Jesus and heaven are really like.

Believe it or not, I'm also thankful for Max the cat, who, like most animals (and people) was right there in front of me, awaiting a touch of love and appreciation.

I think one of the cutest responses Max had to our developing appreciation for him was his feline way of saying "thank you" to us. Most mornings when Max appeared at the back screen and began scratching, he was not alone. When I opened the door, our eyes would meet. Almost immediately Max would look down at the door stoop and redirect my attention to something there. He had brought me the best of the best, in his book: a rodent of some sort lay motionless before me. "Here's my gift of appreciation," Max seemed to say. Then he would meander into the house, leaving his token outside.

The ice-cream shop owners

If you're ever traveling from Syracuse, New York, to the Lake Placid area in the Adirondack Mountains, be sure to stop in the tiny town of Natural Bridge, home to a new and off-the-charts successful ice cream shop, Treats & Tiques. Owned by a mother and daughter and run by their family, this shop offers large, mouthwatering servings of ice cream, shakes, and sundaes. The shop's real success, however, is found in its friendly, welcoming spirit and the love shown to its customers. People line up before the shop opens and linger long past closing because they want more than large helpings of ice cream—their starving souls are fed by these two friendly ladies who share God's grace by living the seven A's.

---

1. *Merriam-Webster's Unabridged Dictionary,* s.v. "appreciation," accessed December 22, 2022, https://unabridged.merriam-webster.com/unabridged/appreciation.

Questions To Ponder

1. What are some simple words that express appreciation?

2. An appreciative person chooses to focus on what qualities of a person, place, or thing?

3. What specific things can you do to develop an attitude of gratitude?

A Word of Appreciation

4. If you are feeling depressed or are in a dark place, for what one or two small things can you express gratitude for? Do you think being grateful will help?

5. If selfishness takes, what do positive words give?

The more appreciation comes out of our mouth and out of the mouths of our those around us, the more our lives are elevated to a higher plane than what most others experience. We are what we digest not only physically, but also emotionally and mentally. Guarding what comes in and aiming at giving thanks as often as we can—for anything and everything—is the antidote to the funks we find ourselves in.

Max was a typical cat. He craved attention! And when he brought us a gift, he would wait to hear the affirmation of what a good hunter he was. Once his petting and praise session ended, he trotted off content, knowing his gift was appreciated! Sometimes a pat on the head works wonders!

Maxism

Loving and giving

is what makes life

worth living!

—Unknown

In Praise of Approval

Let another man praise you, and not your own mouth;
A stranger, and not your own lips. . . .
The refining pot is for silver and the furnace for gold,
And a man is valued by what others say of him.
—Proverbs 27:2, 21

The sixth of our seven A's of God's grace that meets yet another basic need of every human heart is *approval*. Expressing approval is to speak well of someone, to believe that someone or something is good or acceptable.

The approver functions as a "cheerleader." He or she is the one who "brags on" another person. Expressing approval, or praising someone—whether it is a young person, an elderly person, or someone who has behaved admirably—provides positive support.

To express approval is a loving act—so long, of course, as it is not ungodly flattery, which is the devil's counterfeit of approval. And you know that Satan always produces a counterfeit of every good thing.

I remember when I was attending a Christian college in Massachusetts, there was an older teacher there named Mrs. Esteb. Whenever I was in her vicinity, even in a room full of people, she would make a point to come over to me and in some kind, gentle way express her approval. She did the same with other students as well. We all respected and loved Mrs. Esteb.

When I taught my first Bible study, I was terrified. I was painfully shy, and—at eighteen—I was really scared. After it was over, I resolved in my mind that I would never ever do that again. I was certain I had failed miserably. I knew I had been all mixed up and twisted my words and that I had made a complete fool of myself. I felt totally humiliated. But shortly thereafter, I went to my mailbox in the dormitory and found a note from Mrs. Esteb. She wrote "Mike, I am so proud of you! It was wonderful to see one of my students up in front of all those people, teaching and leading. I am praying for you, and I look forward to next week's class."

Mrs. Esteb's simple note expressing approval made me rethink my resolve not to teach a class ever again. She was proud of me! Wow! That was utterly astounding to me. Boy, did that note make me feel good!

Then, lo and behold, it happened again that same week. Dr. Adamson came over to me in biology lab, put his hand on my shoulder, and said, "Mike, I was so proud of you when you were teaching that class on Sabbath. You did a great job teaching the lesson." He said that right there in the lab, in front of my lab partner! Wow! How could I abandon teaching the class after those two caring Christians provided me with such beautiful expressions of approval and encouragement? I couldn't, and I didn't!

What a blessing that experience was for me. What a blessing I would have missed if it hadn't been for Mrs. Esteb and Dr. Adamson. I praise God for their loving ministry to me at a crucial time in my life. Everyone needs an *attaboy* now and then. The approval I got from those two was exactly what I needed to neutralize my pain and emotional insecurity. They were both used as God's instruments. We can be God's instruments too—there are people all around us who need a cheerleader.

Years later, I heard of a man named Freddie Russell, who was pastoring a church called Miracle Temple in downtown Baltimore, Maryland. It was a snowy winter day when Lynn and I went to visit one of his services with our daughter Michelle and son-in-law David. It was so cold and windy, I thought we'd be the only people attending. But as we got close to the church, we found there was no parking nearby—there were cars everywhere!

As we slowly drove around looking for a spot, men from the church approached our car and helped us find a place to park. Then one of those deacons personally escorted us inside and found us a place to sit. It was packed! Everyone we met made us feel welcome. We had never felt so appreciated just for going to church as we did that day. Every deacon and deaconess was an expert in approval. Each one was a cheerleader.

When Pastor Russell got up to speak, he made a point to welcome us, noting that we'd come from out of state on such a cold and windy winter's day.

As good as Pastor Russell's sermon was that day, I can't tell you what it was about. What the four of us will always remember, though, is the love and approval extended to us by him and his church family.

In Romans 15, we find the apostle Paul expressing his sincere approval of the believers in Rome, "Now I myself am confident concerning you, my brethren, that you also are full of goodness, filled with all knowledge, able also to admonish one another" (verse 14). What beautiful words of approval. See how Paul communicates his positive vision of His brethren? Who wouldn't want to be spoken of as Paul speaks in these lovely passages? I know I would.

People followed Jesus because they sensed His love and approval. Where did Jesus get the approval that He shared with others? Can you think of any place in Scripture where we are showed that Jesus received approval? One of the places we are aware of was at His baptism.

Jesus went down into the Jordan River and was submerged in baptism. As He came up out of the water, His heavenly Father said, "This is My beloved Son, in whom I am well pleased" (Matthew 3:17). This is my Boy! I approve of Him!

That was loving approval, wasn't it? It seems likely at that particular moment in His life, Jesus especially needed audible emotional support from His Father who loved Him dearly.

Shortly after hearing His Father's expression of approval, Jesus was led by the Holy Spirit into the wilderness, where He fasted for forty days. Then, when he was in a weakened and vulnerable condition, He was tempted by the devil three times. Amazingly, He met each temptation with a "thus saith the Lord" (Matthew 4:1–11). I believe that during His wilderness trial and His horrendous temptation experience, Jesus heard His Father's voice echoing in His mind and heart. I believe His Father's sweet affirmation at His baptism helped keep Him strong in His time of great crisis. Our approving and encouraging words can strengthen our family and friends and neighbors through their times of difficulties and trials.

Jesus again received an audible expression of approval from His Father toward the end of His earthly ministry. This occurred when He was on a mountain with Peter, James, and John, and His appearance was changed to show His radiant glory (called the Transfiguration). In Matthew 17:5, we read that once again the Father said, "This is My beloved Son, in whom I am well pleased." But this time He added two more words: "Hear Him!"

How wonderful that God provided special strength to His beloved Son by audibly expressing His approval just before He knew that Jesus was about to encounter particularly difficult trials.

If Jesus, the Son of God, needed expressions of approval and affirmation that He was accepted and loved, how much more do we also? You and I and everyone around us could use a cheerleader.

All of us need someone to take the time to write to us, speak to us, and pray for us. We all need caring people to encourage us to remain strong when temptation comes knocking at our door. Could God be beckoning you and me to be that approving voice that says, "I believe in you," "I know you can make it, by God's grace," "You can be assured that I will be there for you day or night, during the thick and thin of life's journey," or "You can count on God and me."

There have been a number of stories in the news over the past few years that highlight the human need for approval as well as the destructive force of inappropriate expressions of disapproval or denunciation, which are the obvious opposites of approval. In these stories we learn of young people who have been the victims of bullies. Sometimes this bullying happens directly and privately between the bully and the victim. Sometimes it takes place more publicly, such as on social media sites or on internet blogs. The result of these terrible expressions of disapproval directed at others has sometimes been tragic. Young people have taken their own lives because they could no longer endure the disapproval heaped upon them by the cruelty of bullies.

I can't help but wonder where those tragic victims of bullying might have been if they each had a cheerleader who expressed strong and loving approval of them every day. This is serious business, my friends. We might not think of expressing approval of others as a life-or-death matter, but the facts suggest otherwise.

Expressions of approval are desperately needed where depression, suicide, addiction, abuse, spousal infidelity, rebellious children, abandonment, and other negative and destructive behaviors are involved.

In Praise of Approval

Both the rebellious person and the victims of such rebellion need to know they are loved and will not be abandoned. Expressing approval during these difficult circumstances must come through God's loving guidance. Every soul is dear to Jesus and should be to us, too.

Look at the example Jesus provided when He spoke with Peter after that impetuous disciple denied knowing His Savior three times. Did Jesus confront and condemn Peter? No. Did Jesus even mention the three denials? No. All Jesus did was lovingly guide Peter into declaring his love for Him. Do you think Peter understood that Jesus loved and approved of him? I am certain he did. Jesus grieves over the sin, but He loves the sinner. He is our example in this as in every other thing. We are to reflect His love and approval and share His grace even with the most unlovable and unlovely.

Always remember the promise in Zephaniah 3:17, which says,

> "For the LORD your God is living among you.
>   He is a mighty savior.
> He will take delight in you with gladness.
>   With his love, he will calm all your fears.
>   He will rejoice over you with joyful songs" (NLT).

God is our greatest cheerleader!

Who are you cheering on through the trials and challenges of life? Do they know you are there for them? Have you told them? Have you written to them so they may gain strength from your words of approval? May we all heed God's voice. May we all demonstrate our Christian love and approval of the people within our sphere of influence. This is surely God's will for each of us.

God the Father, the Son, and the Holy Spirit are all rooting for you. They watch over us every hour of every day. Sometimes, in times of particular difficulty, I keenly sense that there are angels helping me! Remind your family, friends, children, and grandchildren of the precious fact of God's constant protection.

Don't let a day go by without telling someone that they are your beloved son, friend, parent, brother, sister, or spouse, and that you are well pleased with them. I did this for Max verbally every time I saw him, and I gave him a head rub to reinforce it. We humans need verbal and written head rubs too! It feels good and helps our day to go more smoothly and better. Expressing disapproval should only occur in the most critical circumstances and when it is absolutely necessary, which sometimes is the case. Regardless of the circumstances, however, disapproval of a deed must always and only be expressed in love, which leads us directly to our last A.

How do you give a cat "approval"? I've thought long and hard about that. Cats have all kinds of personalities and expressions. But communicating approval to Max was a challenge. I finally just decided I'd adopt the attitude that Max was going to do most things "right." I would approach him with my mind filled with positive thoughts and words, demonstrating calm and casual body language. He was not a destructive, furniture-scratching, chewing kind of cat. We were definitely grateful about that! There was the occasional accident, but he was a relatively good cat (except for his biting, scratching, and snarly attitude when feeling threatened). So approval for Max came through tone of voice, gentle touch, food, water, treats, and respect for his daily routine. Simple, yet satisfying!

The health-food store owner

Lynn and I met a young lady who opened a health food store in a small town in Maine. The establishment took off like a rocket and was quickly very successful. The other two competing stores in town closed their doors after a couple of years. It wasn't because the new store had better food or cheaper prices but because its owner had a million-dollar smile and a God-like personality. She welcomed everyone and always practiced the seven A's. When her customers walked into the store, they felt important. They were noticed, accepted, affirmed, and appreciated. Everyone was seen as a person with a name, not just a purse or wallet.

If Lynn and I are within ten or twenty miles of that place, our need for attention and affection seems to turn our steering wheel in that direction. We find ourselves walking through that health food store's doors—not really needing the food but looking for a warm hug and a cheery hello. We always leave with some health food anyway, but more importantly, we leave with our emotional love cups overflowing with joy, peace, and contentment.

In Praise of Approval

Questions to Ponder

1. Who are the people in your life that you are comfortable going to when you need an emotional lift?

2. When have you responded to people by being a cheerleader and comforter? How did that experience impact you?

3. Are you known as one who rejoices with those who rejoice, and weeps with those who weep? If not, what unfilled needs in your life are holding you back?

4. When you find yourself more in your "heady" than your "hearty," what can you do to move from your head to your heart when giving comfort, encouragement, and strength to others?

A person who approves others is a cheerleader. Everyone needs a cheerleader! I am human! There are times when I need help finding hope. When I am at my lowest, when I am beaten down, God places cheerleaders in my life that reach out to me and affirm me in my humanity. These divine helpers read between the lines of my life and provide what I need to keep walking, while offering the grace of continued approval.

I am not a cat whisperer, and I have no idea what goes on in a cat's head, but Max certainly must have felt the need for approval, and when he received it, there was evidence that his life was changed for the better. I want to be a cheerleader for God—how about you?

MAXism

Bold prayers honor God, and God honors bold prayers.

—Mark Batterson

I Love, Therefore I Admonish

Admonish one another.

—Romans 15:14

The last, but not the least, of the seven A's of God's grace that we are all in need of at one time or another is *admonishment*. The dictionary tells us that to admonish is "to indicate duties, obligations, or requisite action to (a person) . . ." or "to express a direction or explanation or give advice or encouragement to especially in friendly earnest counsel."[1]

Grace-based admonishment is positive, not negative. It is constructive guidance. It involves approaching a friend and telling them of some danger that you—in your understanding and experience—perceive is just around the corner for them if they are not cautious, and you care enough about them to warn them and spare them the heartache.

When you have established a relationship with a person that incorporates the six preceding As (attention, acceptance, affection, affirmation, appreciation, and approval), the seventh A is usually welcomed and your words will fall upon receptive hearts and listening ears. You will receive the thanks and appreciation of your friends when you approach them with tears in your voice and gentle Christ-like love in your heart. Indeed, the apostle Paul says in Romans 15:14 that friends in God should admonish one another.

Max the Cat

Max the cat occasionally needed to be admonished. Since our relationship was loving and filled with the preceding six As of God's grace, eventually he came to obey the command without any fuss. But that wasn't Max's initial response. He came into our home with an attitude! That attitude could have been summed up in these words: "You mess with me, and I'll get even and mess with you." Thankfully, the love and praise of Jesus melted his stubborn and rebellious spirit. The saying "love begets love" is true.

My wife Lynn, like most women I have known, has a sixth sense that most men seem to be missing. When she speaks with warning in her voice or with urgency, I have learned to take immediate notice. Her heavenly intuition is right on target. It took me years to recognize the value and importance of her wise admonishment. Sadly, I, like many men, am sometimes too proud to listen—at least I was for the first twenty or more years of our marriage. When I was finally able to swallow my pride and really listen to my loving wife, I grew to appreciate her admonishment. By listening to her and heeding her counsel, I have been spared untold tragedy, heartache, and embarrassment.

Admonishment usually comes from God through a caring and loving friend or relative. Do yourself and your future a favor by listening and by being grateful for the counsel and guidance proffered by one whom you know speaks from wisdom and experience and from a heart of love. I thank and praise God for my loving and wise wife and for loving and wise friends and co-workers who have cared enough to admonish me along my journey.

We need to care enough to take the time to admonish one another. We need to be thoughtful and diligent to warn our loved ones and friends when we become aware of danger they may not perceive or have chosen to ignore. Many will hold back, asking themselves, *Is this worth losing a friend over?* The real question should be, *Is this worth it if it saves someone who is about to destroy lives—their own and those of the people around them?* God will answer this question for you if you ask Him.

I've watched scores of men foolishly get sucked into a poor business deal, an unwise financial investment, or a stupid affair with a cute chick that ruined two marriages, numerous successful businesses, and many children's lives and futures. Parents cautioned, spouses pled, and friends admonished—all to no avail. Sad!

Admonishment may be an expression of disapproval of something in another person's life. When this is the case, be sure the expression of disapproval or correction is directed toward the action or occurrence, not the person. This is very important!

Never forget to look beyond the deed to the need. This is a hard thing to do unless we have God's help. Humanly, we focus on deeds. When negative and downright ugly or evil words or acts are directed our way, our self-preservation rises up. Our carnal nature automatically wants to fight back. Then, many times, senseless arguments ensue.

Proverbs 15:1 tells us that a soft answer turns away wrath. A soft answer looks beyond the deed to the needy, hurting, broken person you are dealing with. Without Christ and His grace inhabiting us, we naturally fight fire with fire. We must be sure Jesus is on the throne of our lives. He is the only One who reacts with compassion and sympathy to those who live in a world of shame, blame, and judgment. Cry out to God at the beginning of the day, and in difficult moments, ask Him help you to react as Jesus would. This is the Godly way. Stay calm, cool, collected. You will be amazed at the outcome. You will see a miracle take place right in front of you.

There is a saying that goes like this: "A relationship is more important than holding a grudge." I could say, "A relationship is more important than yelling back," or, "A marriage is more important than always being right and having the last word." Remember, we human beings—all of us—are messed up and dysfunctional.

We're the products of many generations of messed up, dysfunctional people who have passed down selfishness, pride, self-pity, evil surmising, loose tongues, and desperate, wicked hearts, to mention a few of the un-Godlike traits in our nature.

Christ is the only solution to our sinful-nature problems. Heaven's grace—and it alone—is eager to forgive us, save us, and transform us if we choose to let it happen. Heaven's grace can help us see, with Heaven's eyes, the person acting out in front of us who needs the seven A's far more than chastisement for their out-of-control and destructive behavior. May God give us the heart and mind of Jesus to respond to those around us who need a loving word of warning or reprimand.

The opposite of admonishment is shaming, blaming, and judging. *Shaming* is telling someone they are so messed up that they are not only wrong but also probably beyond fixing. *Blaming* is telling someone they are responsible for a wrong that has been done. *Judging* is to infer, think, or hold an opinion or conclude something about another, often regarding some real or perceived wrong. These are far from being gracious and loving and kind thoughts, words, and attitudes. No person following and emulating Christ will ever blame or shame or judge any of God's precious children.

Unfortunately, shaming, blaming, judging, and criticizing others heavily outweighs admonishment in our world today. When Christ lives within, people will be positive rather than negative when talking about or to others and will lift others up rather than tear them down. As my friend, Rick, has reminded me many times over the years, "Choose to be kind over being right, and you will be right every time."

Remember, without the preceding six As of God's grace within your relationship with the person you are admonishing, most people will not heed your counsel and will leave with a rebellious and resentful attitude. It goes back to the old school teacher's adage, which applies as well to home, church, the workplace, and wherever we interact with people: "Rules without relationship lead to rebellion."

Most people resent being told what to do or change unless there is a positive, healthy relationship between the two parties, and many of us have learned the truth of this the hard way. This is why many people are angry with or estranged from family or friends. They respond, "Who are you to jump all over me when you have so much dirt in your own backyard?"

Join me in asking God for some of His abundant, limitless, and selfless grace to share with others—especially with those who have only known disgrace. Grace for disgrace is Heaven's "better way." Since God is extremely rich in both grace and mercy (Ephesians 1:7, 2:4), there is plenty to go around. He asks us to come boldly to Him because He has an abundance to share (2 Corinthians 9:8).

Wouldn't it be nice to react to frowns with smiles, to ugliness with kindness, to evil deeds with good deeds? This is the Sermon on the Mount in action. Take time to reread Matthew 5, 6, and 7 and 1 Corinthians 13, and then daily ask God for His love and grace to live like Jesus rather than the adversary.

I'm sure you've seen the reaction on someone's face when you scowl and speak gruffly to them, in contrast to positive encouragement in an uplifting tone of voice. I'm not referring to speaking firmly, with strong direction, at needed moments, but rather the demeaning sarcasm and put-downs that can flow out of our mouths, deflating the listener. Max seemed to know when he was "in the wrong" and needed redirection. However, whenever our voices had that nasty tone woven into the words, his eyes and even his whole body took on a self-protective attitude. His reaction was almost an attack mode. He became defensive only when he was startled or backed into a corner. We learned: Speak the truth and speak it in love.

After his two-year stay with Lynn and me in North Carolina, when Max looked at me, I could almost read in his eyes, hear in his purring, and feel in his body language these thoughts: "Thanks for sharing Heaven's love and grace with me through the seven A's of God's guide to healthy relationships. His TLC (tender love and care) as lived out in these seven A's has changed a stubborn, self-centered, biting, clawing, yet very cute cat into an affectionate, contented, cuddly companion. Thanks, Gram and Gramps!"

A "good Samaritan" farmer

After living in Kansas for nearly three years, I received a phone call from Syracuse, New York, almost one thousand miles away. Lynn and I were invited to do the same jobs there, me running and directing Camp Cherokee's youth camp at beautiful Saranac Lake, in the Adirondack Mountains, with Lynn as camp nurse. It took me all of two seconds to say, "Yes!"

I loved upstate New York—the place where I grew up, pastored five churches, and had served as camp pastor (and Lynn as camp nurse) some eight years earlier. My mom, sister, and extended family lived there, and I was eager to accept that invitation. It's easy to say yes but a much different thing altogether to move, lock, stock, and barrel. After all, we had a house to sell—and two horses, two goats, a dog and a cat to take with us.

By this time, we were learning to lean on and trust in God more completely. We were also learning to "walk by faith, not by sight" (2 Corinthians 5:7). So I bought a small horse trailer, and we loaded it and another makeshift trailer and two cars, and off we headed—five Ortels and seven animals.

All went well until the sun went down and we needed a motel. It was then that I learned that motel owners take people but not horses or goats. I reasoned with the owner of the motel we had chosen, telling him I would tie the horses to a tree overnight and leave the goats in the trailer. His answer: "No way!"

I had been praying but now I was earnestly pleading, "God, I'm tired, my family is tired, and our horses cannot stay all night in our little horse trailer."

Then the motel owner unexpectedly offered, "Even though it's eleven at night, I have a farmer friend I can call and ask if he could be a good Samaritan and help you out."

So off I went into the country with my family and our farm menagerie.

Although all the lights were off, I knocked on the door of the farmhouse about five miles from the motel. Lynn and I kept praying. Soon the upstairs window opened and a bare-chested farmer stuck his head out. He told us to hold on and he'd come down.

Eight minutes later, he appeared and took me to a big free-stall pen next to his cows. He helped me get our horses and goats into his barn, where he gave them hay, water, and grain. Thirty minutes after arriving, we were headed back to the motel.

After a good night's sleep and a hearty breakfast, off we went to the farm. The farmer was again congenial. He helped Shelly and me load our rested-up and well-fed horses and goats.

"What do I owe you?" I asked.

"Nothing," he replied. "Just drive safe and enjoy your new adventure."

What a blessing to meet another good-hearted farmer, like Danny! These men were not interested in money, only in meeting the needs of people—and animals too! They lived the Golden Rule: "Do to others whatever you would like them to do to you" (Matthew 7:12, NLT).

For excellent reading on what Jesus has to say about us Christians "doing good," the following short reading (Luke 6:27–38) is a must. Read it five days in a row, and you will never be the same—your joy quotient in life will grow exponentially!

> "But I say to you who hear: Love your enemies, do good to those who hate you, bless those who curse you, and pray for those who spitefully use you. To him who strikes you on the one cheek, offer the other also. And from him who takes away your cloak, do not withhold your tunic either. Give to everyone who asks of you. And from him who takes away your

goods do not ask them back. And just as you want men to do to you, you also do to them likewise.

"But if you love those who love you, what credit is that to you? For even sinners love those who love them. And if you do good to those who do good to you, what credit is that to you? For even sinners do the same. And if you lend to those from whom you hope to receive back, what credit is that to you? For even sinners lend to sinners to receive as much back. But love your enemies, do good, and lend, hoping for nothing in return; and your reward will be great, and you will be sons of the Most High. For He is kind to the unthankful and evil. Therefore be merciful, just as your Father also is merciful.

"Judge not, and you shall not be judged. Condemn not, and you shall not be condemned. Forgive, and you will be forgiven. Give, and it will be given to you: good measure, pressed down, shaken together, and running over will be put into your bosom. For with the same measure that you use, it will be measured back to you" (Luke 6:27–38).

The more you call on God for His grace—His favors, gifts, blessings, and miracles that you don't deserve and can't earn—the more your faith, trust, joy, and peace will grow. At the same time, your fears, torments, worries, and stress will diminish.

God specializes in the grace business. He loves to give good gifts.

---

1. *Merriam-Webster's Unabridged Dictionary*, s.v. "admonish," accessed December 22, 2022, https://unabridged.merriam-webster.com/unabridged/admonish.

Questions To Ponder

1. Are there people in your early life who gave you positive guidance in a friendly, loving way? Who were they?

2. What was the most impactful guidance or encouragement you received from them?

3. Who are the people in your life today that provide positive guidance, counsel, and encouragement?

4. Are there people in your life today that you can offer positive guidance, counsel, and encouragement to? How can you be intentional in reaching out to them?

Everyone needs a counselor, a person of wisdom, a guide as they go through life. My life is filled with precious counselors and guides that have walked with me and offered encouragement.

Admonishment is not an everyday experience, but it is a powerful positive work done with a heart of love and with the intention of helping us be better.

Max the cat was not an admonisher per se, but he was able to let me know when I was not caring for him in the way he preferred or needed! No matter what the interaction, I was sure to learn something new, and our relationship improved because of it.

Maxism

When you lift others up, God will lift you up. When you take time to make somebody else's day, God will make your day.

—Unknown

Living the Seven A's

I will forever be grateful for the time I had with our grand-cat, Max, and for all the wonderful people God has placed in my life (and me in theirs) over the past three-quarters of a century. There are so many people who have graced me with their kind and loving attention, acceptance, affection, affirmation, appreciation, approval, and admonishment. Their words and actions have given me an abundance of stories that explain and exemplify the seven A's! Many are included in previous chapters of this book. Here are a few more that I hope will inspire you, my dear readers, to play an active role in creating and sustaining healthy and rewarding relationships, sharing your God-given grace with others you meet along your journey.

Danny

Many years ago, when our children were small, we lived in Kansas. I was running and directing youth camps in Kansas and Nebraska for the summer, and Lynn was employed as camp nurse.

Our daughter, Shelly, who was eleven at the time, found herself around many horses, and she fell in love with those big, beautiful animals. By the end of that ten-week summer program, she was begging us for a horse. We had no extra money for a horse, but we knew we had a Father in heaven who owns "the cattle on a thousand hills" (Psalm 50:10).

Shelly begged us and prayed, and soon we traded an old car plus $75 for an old nag and a young, untrained colt.

The camp delivered the horses to our one-acre plot of land in the country, and I soon realized we needed more land for the horses to graze. We prayed. Almost immediately, our neighbor, farmer Danny, made a house call.

He said, "I noticed you have two horses and no pasture. I've got forty acres of pasture all around your house, with only a few beef cows that could use some company. I welcome you to pasture your horses with my cows. Then when winter snows come, I'll bring you a big round bale of hay for your horses."

Lynn, Shelly, and I were in shock with this good news!

I asked Danny, "What do we owe you?"

He looked at us and replied, "Nothing."

"Nothing?" we asked.

"Nothing," he repeated.

We could only say, "Thank you, Danny! And thank you, Father in heaven!"

Upon writing these words for this book, I went to my knees and again thanked my heavenly Father for the hundreds and thousands of gifts and miracles with which He has blessed us. And I remembered these oft-quoted words: "God loves to take ordinary people and do extraordinary things to them and through them."

That's grace! That's God! That's our Father in heaven who delights to give good gifts to His children who ask! God loves to shower all His children with good gifts, just as He did for our Shelly all those years ago.

The lady from Chicago

The trail parking lot for Camelback Mountain in Phoenix, Arizona, is about two and a half miles from my house, convenient enough that I climb the trail twice a week. Over the years, I've met hundreds of people going up and down that path. Some get a thumbs up, others get a kind word, and a few get a touch—everyone gets a smile and a greeting.

On one hike, I greeted a young lady who looked depressed. As we walked together, I asked where she was from and why she was in Phoenix.

Living the Seven A's

She told me she was from Chicago. I made a humorous comment about Chicago that usually elicits a laugh and gets a conversation going. But this lady didn't laugh or even smile.

"I'm here," she said, "because my family and friends advised me to leave the snow and cold in Chicago. I'm depressed, and they thought a change in weather, scenery, and environment would help me get out of the funk I'm in."

I asked her why she was depressed.

"My little dog died," she replied, "and I can't stop grieving." She showed me photos on her phone. She wept and told me life without her dear companion was not worth living.

I told her, "I'm so sorry for you and your loss. It must be so painful." I tried to console her, responding to her sorrow with a kind and tender heart, "I know there must be another dog somewhere in Chicago who is lonely and needs an owner like you. You have love, and that dog needs love."

We chatted more, then we prayed. We ended with a hug and a friendly farewell.

One year later—almost to the day—I was back on Camelback Mountain, jogging a short stretch and heading around a bend, when I heard a loud voice cry, "Stop! Stop!" I was sure the cry wasn't intended for me, so I kept moving. Then I heard a louder voice shout, *"Stop! Stop!"*

So I stopped and looked back. A frantic-looking lady about forty feet behind me motioned for me to come to her. When I reached her, she asked, "Do you remember me?"

It took me less than ten seconds to respond, "You're the Chicago lady!"

"Yes!" she said, and went on to tell me she had gone back to Chicago, found a dog who needed a home, and adopted it. She showed me photos on her phone of the new love of her life. She said she came back to Phoenix to find me and thank me for saving her life by encouraging her to find a new furry friend to love and care for. The day we met up again was the last day before she was to fly back to Chicago.

These two meetings, a year apart, were neither coincidental nor accidental. God providentially connected the dots and brought us together.

Make my life a blessing

Lynn and I encounter people everywhere that we're sure God has arranged for us to meet. They may be young, old, sad, depressed, lonely—all in need of something we have to share because of what He has given us.

Opportunities to bless others pop up at home and abroad. Lynn has met two neighborhood ladies whom she greeted, befriended, and eventually led to give their hearts to Jesus. One was a single mother who worked in a bar; the other, the mother of three girls, drove a school bus for a living. Both needed the seven A's and responded by falling in love with the Giver of all grace. Another time I saw a female airline attendant kneeling by Lynn's seat, gleaning bits of the love and grace God gave to my wife's heart that morning during her devotional time that Lynn passed on to the attendant.

God will send people your way if you are willing to allow Him to love others through you. Say, "God, I am ready for You to use me as your representative today. Send me. Equip me. Bless me to make a huge difference in someone's life today."

Living the Seven A's

Questions To Ponder

It is important to remember the positive stories that impacted your life.

1. Who are four people who have been full of grace and love that have demonstrated the seven A's toward you and made you a better person? How are you a better person because of their influence on your life?

Plus One:
The Importance of Apologizing

Let no corrupt word proceed out of your mouth....
Let all bitterness, wrath, anger, clamor, and evil speaking be put away
from your mouth.... and be kind to one another, tenderhearted,
forgiving one another, even as God in Christ forgave you.
Ephesians 4:29, 31, 32

This book has been finished for several months now. The manuscript has been sent out to a few scholars, friends, and family members, whose reviews I have considered and adopted. So now what do I do with *Max the Cat*.

My editor and I chatted, prayed, and waited for the next step in getting *Max the Cat* printed. Everything was quiet; nothing happened. I've never written a book before. What should I do next? To whom should I speak? Do I need to pray harder? Begin a fast? Then the devil began to send waves of negative thoughts through my mind:

It will never be published.
You're too old and dumb for a writing project like this.
You're not a writer.
No one will want to read it.
It will never help anyone.
Who cares?
Forget the whole thing!
Just retire and play golf or plant a garden.

Then I remembered all the people whose stories had influenced my life for good. Bible characters such as Moses, Gideon, Abraham, and Jehoshaphat. The apostles Peter and Paul and their widespread ministries, and John's witness while imprisoned on the Isle of Patmos. Plus, the super-star ladies of the Bible: Queen Esther, Rahab, Mary Magdalene, and Mary, the mother of Jesus. My own mom, who raised and loved many children, ranks right up there, too. The stories of Abe Lincoln, Norman Cousins, Martin Luther King Jr., and Zig Ziglar made a difference in my life, as have the stories of friends like Harry Williams, James Snoberger, Don Chen, Don John, and so many others—many of whom are mentioned in this book. All these people, like me, were tempted to give up, to forget it. At one time or another, they—like me—wondered, *"Who cares?"*

Then another thought—one I believe was planted there by the Holy Spirit—began rolling around my mind: *There is an Eighth A.* While the seven A's are vital and useful, they are not complete without the eighth: Apology.

There has only ever been one completely perfect person: Jesus. Everyone else came into this world with a sinful nature that has influenced us to hurt people, lie to people, have hateful thoughts about people, and want to get even with people. From time to time, all of us have blown it. Without help from God and from the positive people He puts in our path, we would all live hopeless, helpless, hell-bound, unfulfilled, and pointless lives filled with broken (and heartbreaking) relationships.

All of us have knowingly or unknowingly messed up in a relationship and caused someone to feel hurt. Hurt so easily turns to hate. Walls go up, and bitterness festers and grows. Marriages and families fall apart. Life's promises, hopes, and dreams go out the window. Churches split. Businesses fail. Mental and emotional health problems increase.

What can change all this? The Bible has an answer: Apologize!

A truth discussed often in this book is that wounded people wound people, hurt people hurt people, broken people break people, and abused people abuse people. But it is also true that healed people heal people, helped people help people, and forgiven people forgive people. And thankfully, grace-filled people extend grace to people.

God saw it all coming. The origin of "apology" is not human but rather divine. Grace is divine, meaning it is a heavenly healing gift God is eager to give to all who ask for it. It is free, and God longs to give it away to anyone with a humble, receptive, selfless attitude—which is itself

Plus One: The Importance of Apologizing

divine (Isaiah 30:18,19, NIV). Apology is an aspect of God's grace. (See Hebrews 4:16; John 3:16; Matthew 6:12; Proverbs 1:7; 10:12, 13:10, 12:15, 17:17, 18:21; Ephesians 4:29, 31, 32.)

Apology begins with the feeling of regret God gives us through our conscience, which has been pricked by the Holy Spirit. It is a feeling of remorse, guilt, or sadness that lets us know we may be responsible, in part or in whole, for this mess of brokenness, hurt, and anger.

Our stubborn, selfish, sinful, prideful nature fights off God's wooing to apologize. It rationalizes what it does not want to admit—that maybe *I* am wrong or have something to do with the problem. The more God's Spirit whispers or shouts, our human self resists: *No, no, no! It's not my fault! I can't admit anything or make any apology because it will change how people see me!* All of us have a little bit of narcissism that does not want to admit culpability, and we must have God's help in order to surrender to His still, small voice.

Apology is more than regret; it is the lubricant that we need to keep our relationships growing, healthy, holy, happy, and positive. Without apologies, relationships invariably cool and may quickly become filled with bitterness, resentment, hatred, negativity, or hostility.

Why is it so hard for us to apologize? After all, everyone makes mistakes.

Our selfishness, stubbornness, and pride prevent us from apologizing, resulting in the turmoil we and our world are in today. Adam and Eve messed up. They then ran and hid from God. Instead of going to God and confessing their mistake, they rationalized, pointing away from themselves and placing the blame on the serpent, each other, and even God. (See Genesis 3:8–13.)

Our stubborn, sinful nature separates, gets even, refuses to admit and accept blame. Apologies, on the other hand, have the potential to reunite, heal hurts, end bitterness, and express sorrow for wrongs done (or perceived). Apologies are God's heavenly oil, applied when self and pride are humbled and Satan is ordered to leave. Apologies begin with confession and can lead to forgiveness.

Consider these truths—these texts are pertinent to understanding this process:

> "If we confess our sins, He is faithful and just to forgive us our sins and to cleanse us from all unrighteousness" (1 John 1:9).

"Therefore, submit to God. Resist the devil and he will flee from you. Draw near to God and He will draw near to you. Cleanse your hands, you sinners; and purify your hearts, you double-minded. Lament and mourn and weep! Let your laughter be turned to mourning and your joy to gloom. Humble yourselves in the sight of the Lord, and He will lift you up. Do not speak evil of one another, brethren. He who speaks evil of a brother and judges his brother, speaks evil of the law and judges the law. But if you judge the law, you are not a doer of the law but a judge. There is one Lawgiver [God], who is able to save and to destroy. Who are you to judge another?" (James 4:7–12).

"Do not grumble against one another, brethren, lest you be condemned" (James 5:9).

"Confess your trespasses to one another, and pray for one another, that you may be healed" (James 5:16).

"Yes, all of you be submissive to one another, and be clothed with humility, for 'God resists the proud, but gives grace to the humble.' Therefore, humble yourselves under the mighty hand of God, that He may exalt you in due time, casting all your care upon Him, for He cares for you" (1 Peter 5:5, 6).

God wants us to "be the bigger person," to acknowledge and affirm the feelings of others, to let go of our pride and judgmental tendencies—to apologize. He alone can give us the heart and words to do so sincerely.

Apologizing is important, but we often do it wrong. What does a sincere apology look like? It's simple:

I am sorry.
I hurt you.
I was wrong.
I was selfish.
Please forgive me.

Notice that none of these three-word sentences is followed by a "but"—no excuses, no rationalizations, no attempts to place the blame elsewhere. A genuine apology does not attempt to justify my words or

Plus One: The Importance of Apologizing

actions. A genuine apology acknowledges that my words or actions have resulted in another's pain. Period.

An apology is an admission of wrongdoing, requires humility, and opens the door to healing. Yelling, fighting, and proving the other person wrong are not part of God's blueprint. I learned many years ago that it takes emotions to heal emotions. Broken relationships are matters of the heart, where our feelings and emotions are headquartered. Arguments, rationalization, logic, and reason come from the head, not the heart. They never heal—they only make things worse. Satan battles with facts. Jesus offers forgiveness, whether I am 1 percent guilty or 100 percent guilty (1 Corinthians 13:4–8, 16:14; 1 Peter 4:8).

Satan and self fight to win—I am right and you are wrong. With Jesus' help, I accept the blame and humbly acknowledge the hurt I caused, and ask for forgiveness. God's apologizing grace is not interested in who is right or wrong but rather in identifying what hurts I have inflicted that I can attempt to make right.

Jesus died on the cross for you and me so that we might accept His grace and be transformed (changed) here on earth *and* be saved for eternity with Him. Our daily walk and talk will be filled with forgiving and loving and not with arguing and fighting.

The God-given ability to apologize can allow us to sleep better, live happier, enjoy greater mental and emotional health, and embrace Heaven's peace—a peace that passes all human understanding. And—as stated in the Scriptures listed earlier in this chapter—it gives us the assurance of eternal life.

God's grace that allows us to apologize humbly and sincerely is readily available to all who ask. It does wonders in our hearts, our churches, our homes, our neighborhoods, and at work. If we are living with unhealthy, broken relationships with anyone, Jesus makes it clear that we must go to Him first, asking Him for one of His powerful, sweet, miracle-working graces called an apology. He has promised that this divine gift is ours for the asking.

All God's promises have prerequisites: We must come to Him with humility, not pride; with selflessness, not selfishness; with unconditional ("agape") love, not hate. These "prerequisites" are what grace looks like. Sometimes we may feel we just cannot muster up these qualities, but thankfully, if we but ask, God can and will supply what we don't have: "With men this is impossible, but with God all things are possible" (Matthew 19:26).

God has promised to change our self-centered, prideful, sin-filled hearts. All He asks is for you and me to daily surrender to Him—withholding nothing.

Letting go and giving all to God is freeing, liberating, unshackling. The chains of sinful thinking, harmful addiction, and corrupt communication are now broken by His divine bolt cutters. Victories are achieved, relationships are mended, and guilt is gone. By focusing on Him and His amazing promises, you are now a new person. You are born again, changed, saved.

I love to hear the amazing stories of people I have met at Home Depot and Walmart, on airplanes, on my daily hikes or at AA meetings. Some are homeless and penniless; others are corporate tycoons. Many have been divorced, have several children from several relationships, or have spent months or years behind bars. Because of their sins, they have experienced mountains of guilt and highways of heartaches. But they listened and responded as Jesus called them to give it all to Him. In return, He gave them the grace called "apology," and they now live in joy and peace.

I was recently in a church where, just before the sermon, a lady stood up and read the riot act to the full congregation. After she let it all out, I expected either complete silence or a heated argument. The air was thick with tension. Then a tall, dignified man walked to the microphone and said, "I am the guilty one. I did it. I apologize. I won't do it again. I'm sorry. Please forgive me." His public apology was accepted. The tension dissolved, and the congregation sang together a hymn filled with words of peace and praise to God. The heavenly water of apology put out the fire of anger and bitterness.

This incident had the potential for a verbal fight. This incident had the potential for a congregational split. What an example of God's love that gives grace, that leads to apology, that brings peace, unity, and bonding. Thank you, God. Thank you, humble sir. Thank you, forgiving woman.

This is how hurts are healed and problems are resolved. The Christian life is not about being right but rather about being humble, loving, and Christlike.

Another time, I witnessed the end of a thirty-year-long feud. Parents and daughter began a cold war that got worse with each passing year. Both sides were (professed) Christians who lived ten miles apart. Grandparents never saw or spoke to their grandchildren, whom they wanted to know and love.

Plus One: The Importance of Apologizing

One day the guilt became unbearable, and one member of the estranged family wrote an apology letter. It spelled out all the grievances, sin, hurt, pain, and brokenness. It was full of tears, regrets, sadness, confession, and forgiveness. The other side responded with a similar Holy Spirit inspired apology. The two sides got together; they wept and hugged and thanked God for His persistent nudging and inescapable conviction. They now know that the heavenly home God has been preparing for them will be theirs, together, because of these precious words: "I am so sorry. I was wrong. I hurt you. I wanted revenge. Please forgive me. I love you."

Let's make earth a happier place by responding to God's still, small voice. Let's joyfully accept God's invitation to live on earth in peace, loving and forgiving one another. Let's enjoy the full assurance that Heaven will be our eternal home, because we believe and accept that Jesus died for our sins, selfishness, stubbornness, and pride and because we have confessed, apologized, and asked forgiveness from Him and all others we have used, abused, or hurt.

Won't that be a glorious day? Won't that be a glorious reunion when we see and unconditionally "love up on" Him, our Guardian Angel, the Heavenly Father, the Holy Spirit, and all those people with whom, through God's grace, we have restored relationships?

Now, some will read all that has come before and say, "Mike, I've done all you've outlined in this book. I've accepted God's grace and, by His power, done my best to pass it on to the people in my life, practicing all the A's—including apology. And yet. . .my [spouse, child, parent, co-worker, boss, teacher, etc.] still won't speak to me."

The reality is that some relationships will not be restored this side of Heaven, no matter what we do. Doing the right thing does not guarantee a positive outcome. We have no control over the frustrations, anger, hatred, and festering wounds others may bring to the conversation. God only holds us responsible for doing what we know is right, not for how our right-doing is received (James 4:17, Micah 6:8). It is our unquestioning, humble, willing obedience to God that brings us peace, not the outcome of that obedience.

As Art Miller, a dairy farmer and preacher in Brattleboro, Vermont, once said to me, "We win or lose by the way we choose."

Today I choose our amazing Jesus as my Savior and Friend. I choose the seven A's and the hugely important eighth A: apology. I apologize, Jesus, for wounding you and nailing you to the cross, and to the hundreds my earthly brothers and sisters I have knowingly or unknowingly wounded and nailed to the cross because of my sinful, selfish treatment of them.

May God bless us all until we meet on those golden streets of heaven.

Thank you, Max the cat, for teaching me all of the relationship secrets. And Max, I apologize for all the times I stepped on your tail!

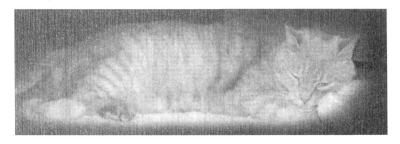

Plus One: The Importance of Apologizing

Questions To Ponder

1. How do you feel when you pour out your heart with a sincere apology?

2. What's the opposite of humility? How has this impacted your life and interactions with others?

3. What are some thoughts, sentences, and words that are in the emotional family of a sincere apology?

Maxism

In every good

relationship there are

two great forgivers!

—Unknown

Additional Resources

Here are a few of the books that I have found inspirational and directional as I have navigated through the many relationships in my life. It is my prayer that you will find them useful as well!

Path to the Heart, by Glenn Coon
Ministry of Healing, by E.G. White
Mount of Blessings, by E.G. White
Intimate Moments, by David and Teresa Ferguson and Chris and Holly Thurman
Experiencing God Day By Day, by Henry and Richard Blackaby
See You at The Top, by Zig Ziglar
Filling Your Love Cup, by Kay Kuzma
Live to 101, edited by Mark Finley and Peter Landless
Called to Prayer, by Jacki Howerin
My Utmost for His Highest, by Oswald Chambers
Belonging, by Drs. Ron and Nancy Rockey and Kay Kuzma

Maxism

Freely you have

received, freely give.

—Matthew 10:8

The Last Word

I hope you have enjoyed reading this book as much as I've enjoyed living it. For me, there is such great reward in watching people leave our conversation with a lighter heart, an encouraged spirit and a renewed authentic smile on their face. As you have started practicing these powerful principles, have you experienced that, too? I sure hope so.

There are some days when being kind, encouraging, and supporting seems just too much of an effort. Our resources seem depleted. Our own hearts need encouraging. That is the real life! You know that you cannot give what you do not have. Yet you want to be a positive contributor to any person you meet.

Perhaps a reminder about the resource of the seven A's and all the good gifts of life is all it takes. There is One who has everything we need. He willingly longs to share it. This Royal Friend is eager to give you His resources for everything you need for a satisfying life—for every day of your life.

Our God invites us to be recipients of all He has to offer. Will you accept? He has plenty for you and more to share! Our God offers you every single "A" plus everything thing else you need—for the asking and accepting!

- Ask Him to help you
- Admit that you need help
- Accept what He offers
- Appreciate His generosity

And then live abundantly, the way He has designed for you! (John 10:10)

Every moment of the day, if needed, you can request His help. You can daily read His promises, advice and encouragement in the Bible. He never wearies sharing His wisdom with you. In fact, He really enjoys your requests! That gives Him glory!

I would like to leave you with this quote from a gentleman that lived a long time ago. It has stayed with me and influenced my life, kept me on the straight and narrow in the hands of God, and gave me hope as I went through the vicissitudes of life. Most people I have given this quote to have been changed, and I want to gift this to you, dear reader, as you journey through the relationships in your world:

"God brings no man into the conflicts of life to desert him. Every man has a friend in heaven whose resources are unlimited; and on Him he may call at any hour and find sympathy and assistance. (Robert H. Morris, Mayor of New York City, 1841–1844)

Have fun connecting with our God for yourself and then sharing His goodness wherever you go! Your life will become a constant fun-filled adventure as you represent Jesus by sharing the "seven A's of healthy relationships"!